Amigurumi Toilet Paper Covers

Cute Crocheted Animals, Flowers, Food, Holiday Decor and More!

Linda Wright

To John and Corrigan, Thank you for showing me life through the eyes of a child.

Also by Linda Wright

Amigurumi Golf Club Covers

Amigurumi Christmas Ornaments

Amigurumi Animal Hats

Amigurumi Animal Hats Growing Up

Honey Pie Amigurumi Dress Up Doll with Picnic Play Set

Honey Bunny Amigurumi Dress Up Doll with Garden Play Mat

Chef Charlotte Amigurumi Dress Up Doll with Tea Party Play Set

Edition 3.0

Lindaloo Enterprises

P.O. Box 90135

Santa Barbara, California 93190

United States

sales@lindaloo.com

ISBN: 978-0-9800923-6-3

Library of Congress Control Number: 2013920784

Contents

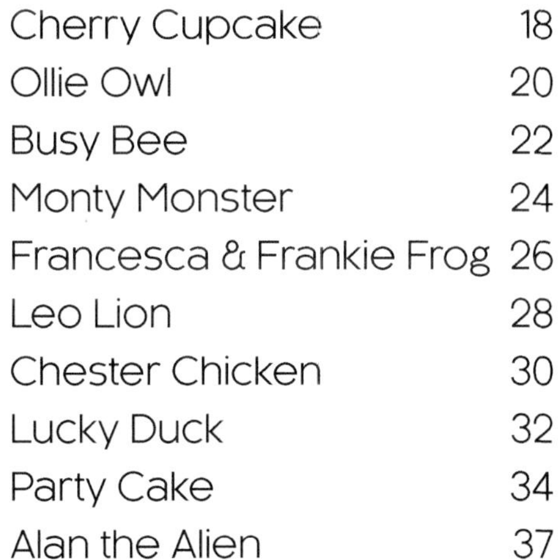

W

Introduction

Keeping a spare roll of toilet paper close at hand has just gotten cuter! Imagine a critter, a cupcake, or a car with a grinning grille covering your auxiliary roll . . . and you'll never want to see bare bath tissue again!

Amigurumi (ah•mee•goo•roo•mee) is a Japanese term for crocheted stuffed toys. They are made by crocheting in the round using one primary stitch—the single crochet. Amigurumi has a widespread reputation for being tons of fun—and totally adorable! No matter how many amigurumi I make, I never fail to smile when the assembly is complete and each creation comes to life.

Amigurumi toilet paper covers are quick and easy to make. These are beginner's level projects, designed to be simple enough that even a novice crocheter can complete the patterns with success.

Amigurumi toilet paper covers are delightful to make for your own bathroom and ideal for gifts. They are practical additions to bathroom decor that will brighten the space with a pop of color, a dollop of whimsy and a touch of cheer. If you enjoy my book, I would appreciate it so much if you leave a review at your online place of purchase. Other customers would appreciate it too!

Let's get rolling!

General Directions

If you're new to crocheting, or if you need to brush up, the following pages include diagrams for the stitches used in this book. If you like to learn by watching, YouTube.com is a treasure trove of excellent tutorials. Just search on the stitch you want to learn. For example, magic ring crochet (also known as the magic circle or magic loop), single crochet, or loop stitch crochet. Several embroidery stitches are used for finishing the toilet paper covers and these can also be found demonstrated on YouTube, for example, chain stitch embroidery and the French knot. For a hand-picked source of tutorials, I have assembled my favorites on Pinterest. You can view them at www.pinterest.com/LindalooEnt/ on boards named "Amigurumi Tutorials" and "Embroidery Tutorials".

Amigurumi is meant to be crocheted rather tightly, so keep that in mind as you work. This will prevent fiberfill from showing through your stitches on any stuffed pieces.

This book uses U.S. crochet terms. If an instruction says sc, that is a U.S. single crochet—or a U.K. double crochet. Please refer to the stitch diagrams on pages 10-14 to be sure you are making the stitches as intended.

Bare Essentials

Toilet Paper Roll

Purchase your favorite "double roll" of toilet paper. The roll size will vary slightly among brands, but a quality double roll measures approximately 4" tall by 4 3/4" diameter by 15" in circumference.

Yarn

All of these projects are made using inexpensive and washable worsted-weight acrylic or acrylic-blend yarn marked as number 4. Look on the label for the yarn weight symbol with a 4 in the middle of a ball of yarn. I primarily use Caron "Simply Soft". Other yarns that I like include Red Heart "Soft Yarn", Lion Brand "Vanna's Choice", Lion Brand "Cotton-Ease", Loops & Threads "Impeccable" (Michaels store brand), and Hobby Lobby "I Love This Yarn" .

For starters, you may want to use the same colors of yarn that I used for these projects, but I encourage you to have fun changing the colors to suit your fancy—or to match your bathroom.

Scissors

You will need a pair of sharp scissors to cut your yarn.

Crochet Hook

All of these projects use a U.S. H/8 (5 mm) crochet hook. Hooks are available in various materials including wood, metal and plastic. The choice is just a matter of personal preference. My absolute favorite is the Clover Soft Touch Crochet Hook (pictured below, center). I love the ergonomic grip which keeps my hand from going numb when crocheting for long periods of time and the shape of the head which inserts easily into a stitch.

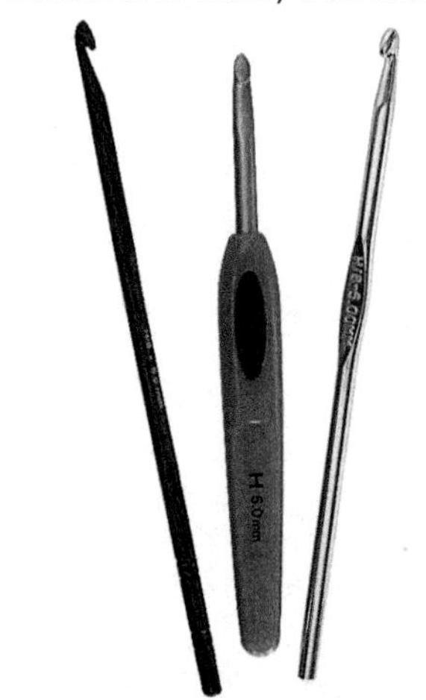

Yarn Needle

Yarn needles, or jumbo tapestry needles, have a large eye and a blunt point. They are made from metal or plastic. You will use one to sew the various pieces of your amigurumi together and also to finish every project by weaving the loose ends into your work.

Stitch Markers

Stitch markers are used to keep track of where a round of crochet begins and ends. You can use a safety pin, bobby pin, paper clip or purchased stitch markers. I recommend the locking stitch markers that are shaped like safety pins. They are very easy and convenient to use. Making the correct number of stitches is important, so count to double check if ever you're not sure.

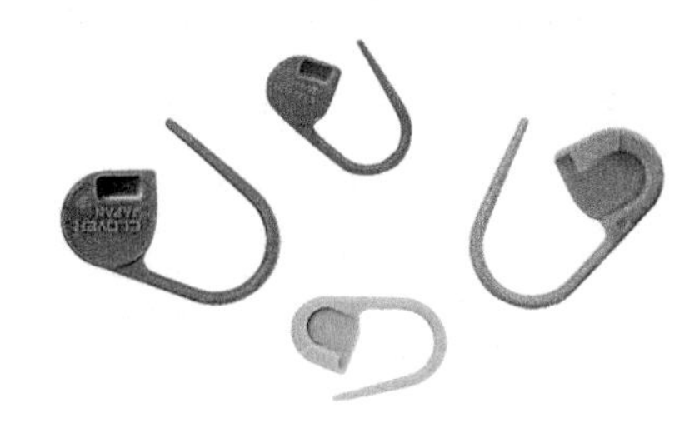

Polyester Fiberfill

While the main portion of your toilet paper cover is stuffed with a roll of TP, the extra little parts, such as legs and snouts, are stuffed with polyester fiberfill. This can be purchased by the bag at craft stores. One bag will go a long way!

Other Supplies

Animal Eyes & Noses

Plastic animal safety eyes and noses work magic in bringing personality and a professional look to your amigurumi. They can be purchased at craft stores or online. My favorite internet sources are "Lisa and Ed's Eye's and More" at lisa.staton.home.insightbb.com and "Etsy Shop 6060" at etsy.com/shop/6060.

Each feature consists of a post section and a washer. To attach, work the post into a gap between stitches. Place the washer against the post, lay eye or nose against a hard surface and press hard.

Note: As an alternative, any ami's eyes can be made from buttons, crocheted circles, or circles of felt sewn into place. Feel free to mix it up to get a look you like.

Wire Cutters

To clip excess post off of safety eyes.

Disappearing Ink Marking Pen

This terrific marking tool is a felt-tipped pen with ink (usually purple) that disappears in a day or so. Purchase it at a fabric store, craft store or online.

Removable Notes

Use sticky notes to keep track of your place in a pattern. Every time you complete a round or a row, move the note down to reveal the next line of instructions. I wouldn't work without one!

Row Counter

Well worth the investment, a row counter keeps track of what round of the pattern you are crocheting. A pencil and paper can also be used.

Sewing Needle & Thread

You will need these sewing box basics when button eyes are used.

Straight Pins

Use standard dressmaker's pins or long corsage pins to hold pieces in place before sewing.

Ruler

For measuring and marking.

Hole Punch

Use to punch paper templates for my connect-the-dots method of marking your work.

Socket Wrench

It can be difficult to push the washer portion of safety eyes onto the post, especially when pushing through multiple layers of fabric. In this case, a socket wrench is a great aid. Choose a socket that is slightly smaller than the diameter of the washer, position the socket and press firmly.

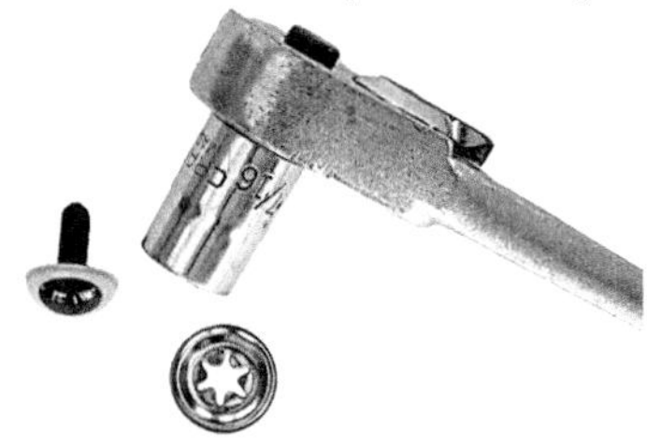

Crochet Stitches

SLIP KNOT

This is used to make a starting loop on the crochet hook.

1. Make a loop about 5 inches from end of yarn. Insert hook in loop and hook onto supply yarn (yarn coming from ball) at A.

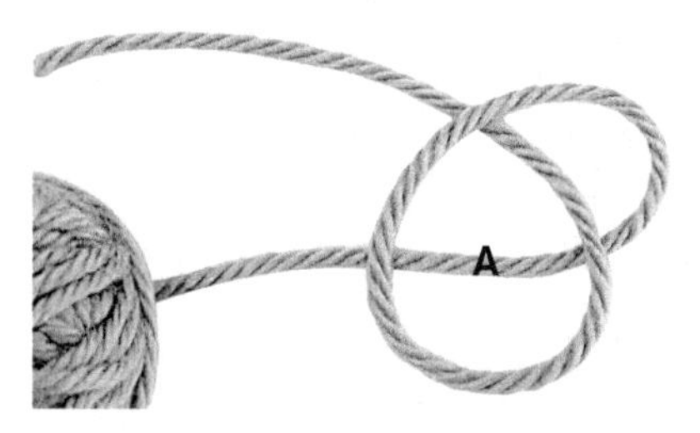

2. Pull yarn through loop.

3. Pull yarn ends to tighten loop around hook.

CHAIN (CH)

Start with a slip knot on hook.

1. Bring yarn over hook from back to front. Catch yarn with hook and pull it through the loop . . .

to look like this. One chain is done.

SINGLE CROCHET (SC)

This simple stitch is the primary stitch for amigurumi.

1. Insert hook in designated stitch. Note: Put hook under both loops that form v-shape at top of stitch unless otherwise instructed.

2. Yarn over and pull up a loop.

You will now have 2 loops on the hook.

3. Yarn over and pull yarn through both loops on hook.

4. You now have 1 loop on hook and the stitch is done.

LOOP STITCH (LP ST)

The Loop Stitch is a variation of single crochet. In this book, it is worked on the wrong side of the fabric because the loops form on the side opposite the side you are facing. By working on the wrong side of your crochet, loops will form on the right side—where you want them.

1. Insert hook in designated stitch, just as you do for a single crochet.

2. Wrap yarn around index finger of your yarn-holding hand to make a loop and lay loop on top of hook. Pull strands A and B through stitch C.

3. Yarn over and pull through all 3 loops on hook—A, B, and C.

4. Stitch is done.

SLIP STITCH (SL ST)

1. Insert hook in stitch. Yarn over and pull through stitch and through loop on hook (A and B).

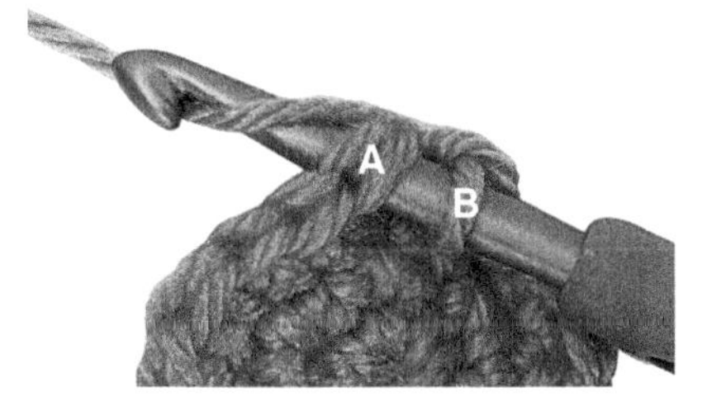

2. Slip stitch is done.

SINGLE CROCHET DECREASE (SC2TOG)

The instruction "sc2tog" means to use single crochet to join 2 stitches together. It is a way to decrease or make the item smaller.

1. Insert hook in stitch, yarn over and pull up a loop . . . to look like this.

2. Insert hook in next stitch, yarn over and pull up a loop . . . to look like this.

3. Yarn over and pull through all 3 loops on hook . . . to look like this. Stitch is done.

Techniques

★MAGIC RING

Most all of my amigurumi begins with the magic ring. This is the way to get a nice, neat center when crocheting in the round. The magic ring is an adjustable loop that you can tighten—like magic! It's not difficult—and well worth it. (An alternative to the magic ring, if desired, is to chain 2. Then begin Round 1 by working into the 2nd chain from the hook instead of the ring.)

1. Make a ring a few inches from end of yarn. Grasp ring between thumb and index finger where the join makes an X. Insert hook in ring, hook onto supply yarn at Y and pull up a loop . . .

to look like this.

2. Chain 1 . . .

to look like this. This chain does not count as a stitch.

3. Insert hook into ring so you're crocheting over ring and yarn tail. Pull up a loop to begin your first single crochet . . .

and complete the single crochet.

4. Continue to crochet over ring and yarn tail for the specified number of single crochets for the 1st round.

5. Pull tail to close up ring. To begin the 2nd round, insert hook in 1st stitch of 1st round (see arrow).

WORKING IN THE ROUND

Working in the round means crocheting in a continuous spiral. Most amigurumi is worked in this manner.

USING STITCH MARKERS

It can be tricky to keep track of your place when working in the round, so be sure to use a stitch marker. The pattern will remind you! Place the stitch marker in the first stitch of a round—after completing the stitch. When you've crocheted all the way around, remove the stitch marker, make the next stitch, and replace the marker in the stitch just made. This will be the first stitch of the next round.

WORKING IN LOOPS

When a single crochet stitch is made, you will see 2 loops in a v-shape at the top of the stitch. Unless instructed otherwise, crochet these patterns by inserting your hook under **both** loops. For special effects, you will occasionally be instructed to work in the **back** loop of a stitch. This creates a cute little ridge.

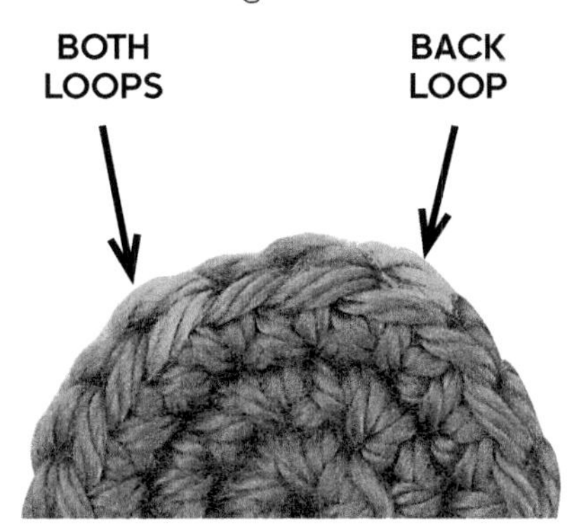

CHANGING COLORS

To change color while single crocheting, work last stitch of old color to last yarn over, yarn over with new color and pull through both loops on hook to complete the stitch.

FASTENING OFF

This is the way to finish a piece so that it won't unravel. When you're done crocheting, cut the yarn and leave a tail. Wrap the tail over your hook and pull it all the way through the last loop left on your hook. Pull the tail tight and it will make a knot.

WEAVING IN ENDS

The final assembly instruction for every project is to weave in the ends. This is the way to hide and secure all of your straggly yarn tails. Thread the yarn end into a yarn needle, then skim through the back of the stitches on the wrong side of your work. Continue for about 2 inches, then turn and double back to lock the yarn into place. Trim the end close. When you turn your work to the right side, you should not see the woven ends. They should be tucked into the middle of your crocheted fabric.

FRINGE

1. Lay strands of yarn together side-by-side. (Refer to your pattern for the length and quantity of strands.) Put hook through desired stitch, catch strands in the middle and pull part way through stitch to make a loop.

2. With hook in loop, lay yarn ends over hook.

3. Pull yarn ends all the way through loop. Take hold of ends and pull tight.

STUFFING

The goal is to stuff firmly without stretching the crochet stitches. Pull a chunk of fiberfill from the package and gently work it into your crocheted piece. Do not wad the fiberfill into a ball or you will get a lumpy look. Sometimes, when stuffing narrow tubes, it is helpful to use a dowel, chopstick or skewer to push the fiberfill into place. When stuffing pieces such as arms, legs and snouts, stuff the piece lightly, just until it holds its shape; then, when you are almost done sewing the piece into position on the Basic Roll Cover, pause to pack in more stuffing before sewing the final stitches.

ASSEMBLING

Thread a yarn needle with matching yarn and whip stitch to join your pieces. Your stitches will be practically invisible. It's good to temporarily pin your pieces in place beforehand to decide where you like them the best.

CLEANING

If you've used washable yarn, your toilet paper cover will be easy to clean. Just follow the care instructions on the yarn label and wash it by machine or hand as recommended. Lay flat to dry.

Embroidery Stitches

STRAIGHT STITCH

A simple, single stitch. Come up from wrong side of fabric at A and go down at B.

RUNNING STITCH

The Running Stitch is formed by a detached series of Straight Stitches. Make it by running the needle up and down the fabric at a regular distance. Come up at A, down at B, up at C, down at D, up at E, down at F, etc.

FRENCH KNOT

Bring needle up from wrong side at A. Place needle close to fabric and wrap yarn around needle 3 times. Push needle down at a point near A.

CHAIN STITCH

1. Bring needle up from wrong side at A. Put needle back in at A and out at B, but don't pull the needle completely through.

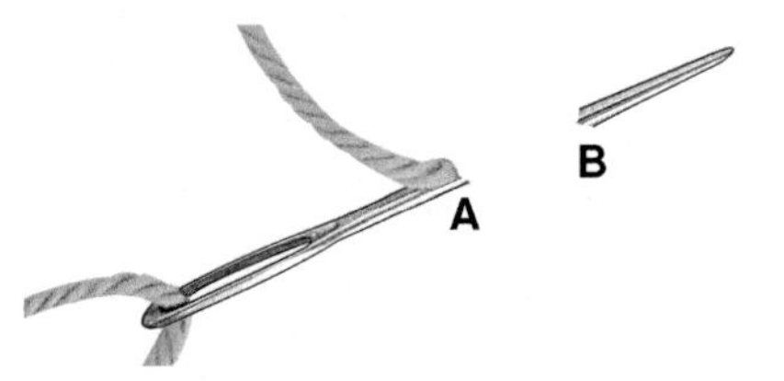

2. Wrap yarn around needle from left to right to form a loop.

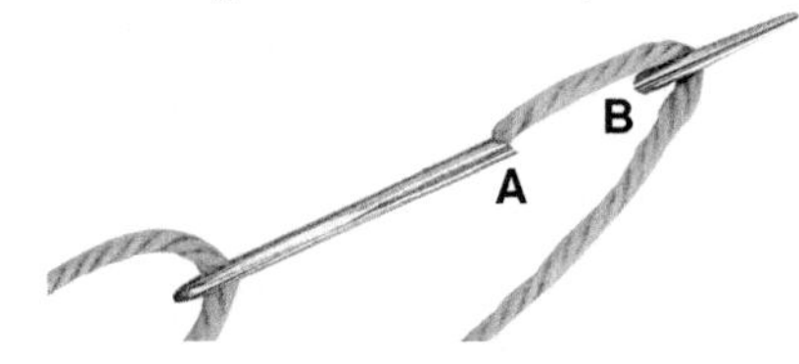

3. Pull needle out to tighten loop. First stitch is done.

4. Put needle in at B, and out at C. Repeat Steps 2 and 3 to complete 2nd stitch. Continue to make as many stitches as needed.

How to Read a Pattern

The following abbreviations are used:

st	stitch
ch	chain
sc	single crochet
sl st	slip stitch
lp st	loop stitch
rnd	round
sc2tog	single crochet decrease
TP	toilet paper
* *	repeat
( )	stitch count

Each round or row is written on a new line. Most rounds have a repeated section of instructions that are written between two asterisks *like this*. The instruction between the asterisks is to be repeated as many times as indicated before you move on to the next step. At the end of a round, the total number of stitches to be made in that round is indicated in parentheses (like this).

Let's look at a round from the Basic Roll Cover:

Rnd 6: *sc in next 4 sts, 2 sc in next st* 6 times (36 sts).

This means:

Rnd 6	This is the 6th round of the pattern.
sc in next 4 sts	Make 1 single crochet stitch in each of the next 4 stitches
2 sc in next st	Make 2 single crochet stitches, both in the same stitch
6 times	Repeat everything between * and * 6 times.
(36 sts)	The round will have a total of 36 stitches.

So, following the instructions for Round 6, you will:

single crochet in the next 4 sts, 2 sc in the next st,

single crochet in the next 4 sts, 2 sc in the next st,

single crochet in the next 4 sts, 2 sc in the next st,

single crochet in the next 4 sts, 2 sc in the next st,

single crochet in the next 4 sts, 2 sc in the next st,

single crochet in the next 4 sts, 2 sc in the next st,

for a total of 36 stitches.

Gauge

Exact gauge is not necessary for these projects. Each Basic Roll Cover is custom-made to fit your toilet paper roll. Keep in mind, however, that amigurumi needs to be crocheted pretty tightly so that the stuffing in stuffed pieces doesn't show through the stitches.

My gauge with an H/8 (5 mm) hook using worsted-weight yarn (Caron Simply Soft) is as follows:

7 Rounds of the Basic Roll Cover = 3" diameter circle

9 Rounds of the Basic Roll Cover = 4" diameter circle

Don't worry if your gauge is different from mine. If your auxiliary features (eyes, ears, nose, etc.) turn out a bit larger or smaller than you like, just change to a smaller or larger crochet hook.

Basic Roll Cover

TOP

SIDE

Every amigurumi toilet paper cover starts with a cylindrical sheath that fits snugly on the toilet paper roll. The Basic Roll Cover is custom-made so that no matter the size of your toilet paper roll, the thickness of your yarn, or the tightness with which you crochet, your cover will fit.

SUPPLIES

Worsted weight yarn 

Refer to pattern for yardage

Size H/8 (5 mm) crochet hook

Toilet Paper Roll (double roll size)

Stitch marker

Yarn needle

TOP

Make a magic ring, ch 1.

Rnd 1: 6 sc in ring, pull ring closed tight (6 sts).

Rnd 2: 2 sc in each st around. Place marker for beginning of rnd and move marker up as each rnd is completed (12 sts).

Rnd 3: *sc in next st, 2 sc in next st* 6 times (18 sts).

Rnd 4: *sc in next 2 sts, 2 sc in next st* 6 times (24 sts).

Rnd 5: *sc in next 3 sts, 2 sc in next st* 6 times (30 sts).

Rnd 6: *sc in next 4 sts, 2 sc in next st* 6 times (36 sts).

Rnd 7: *sc in next 5 sts, 2 sc in next st* 6 times (42 sts).

Rnd 8: *sc in next 6 sts, 2 sc in next st* 6 times (48 sts).

Fitting your Top: At this point, lay the piece on top of your TP roll (over the hole) to check the size. Your goal is to make the Top slightly smaller than the diameter of your TP roll as shown in Figure A. The stitches will stretch to give a secure fit. I usually have a good fit at Rnd 10 (60 sts).

FIGURE A

Toilet Paper Roll

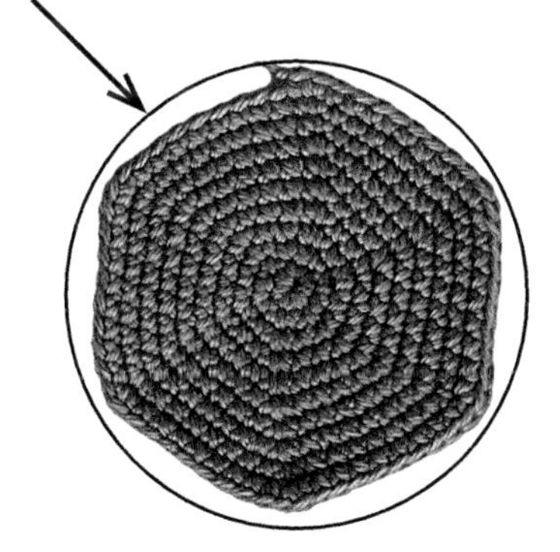

Continue crocheting Top until you get the right size for your TP roll.

Rnd 9: *sc in next 7 sts, 2 sc in next st* 6 times (54 sts).

Rnd 10: *sc in next 8 sts, 2 sc in next st* 6 times (60 sts).

Note: If a larger diameter is needed, repeat Rnd 10, increasing the number of plain sc ("sc in next ___ sts") by one st for each round until the proper size is reached.

SIDE

Continue to Side by crocheting into stitches around edge of Top.

Rnds 1-?: sc in each st around until cover reaches bottom of TP roll. Place marker for beginning of rnd and move marker up as each rnd is completed.

Fasten off.

Note: My typical Basic Roll Cover has 23 Rounds for the Side.

Cherry Cupcake

SUPPLIES

Worsted weight yarn in pink, tan and white (approx. 50 yards each) plus small amount of red, purple, yellow, green and orange

Size H/8 (5 mm) crochet hook

Toilet paper roll

Fiberfill stuffing

Pencil

Stitch marker

Yarn needle

CAKE

Make Basic Roll Cover (see page 17) as follows: For the Top, use white yarn. For the Sides, use white yarn for Rnds 1-6 and tan yarn for the remainder.

FROSTING

With pink yarn, follow instructions for Basic Roll Cover Top and Rnds 1-10 of Sides.

Rnd 11: *5 sc in next st, skip 1 st, sl st in next st* around. Fasten off.

CHERRY

With red yarn, make a magic ring, ch 1.

Rnd 1: 6 sc in ring, pull ring closed tight (6 sts).

Rnd 2: 2 sc in each st around. Place marker for beginning of rnd and move marker up as each rnd is completed (12 sts).

Rnds 3-4: sc in each st around.

Rnd 5: sc2tog, 6 times, stuffing piece midway around (6 sts).

Fasten off with long tail. Pack in more stuffing with eraser end of pencil. Sew opening shut. Sew Cherry to top of Frosting.

SPRINKLES

Embroider French knots on top of Frosting with purple, green, yellow and orange yarn.

ASSEMBLY

Put Cake on toilet paper roll. Stuff Frosting with fiberfill and pin in place to cover white section of Cake. Sew Frosting to Cake, stitching just above scalloped edge so that scallops hang free. Weave in ends. ♦

Ollie Owl

SUPPLIES

Worsted weight yarn in pink and turquoise (approx. 50 yards each) plus small amount of yellow, white and black

Size H/8 (5 mm) crochet hook

Toilet paper roll

2 black buttons, 3/4" diameter (optional)

Stitch marker

Yarn needle

HEAD

Make Basic Roll Cover (see page 17) using pink yarn for Top and Rnds 1-10 of Sides. Use turquoise yarn for the remainder.

INNER EYE (MAKE 2)

Use buttons or crochet as follows.

With black yarn, make a magic ring, ch 1.

Rnd 1: 6 sc in ring, pull ring closed tight (6 sts).

Sl st in next st. Fasten off with long tail.

OUTER EYE (MAKE 2)

With white yarn, make a magic ring, ch 1.

Rnd 1: 6 sc in ring, pull ring closed tight (6 sts).

Rnd 2: 2 sc in each st around. Place marker for beginning of rnd and move marker up as each rnd is completed (12 sts).

Rnd 3: *sc in next st, 2 sc in next st* 6 times (18 sts).

Rnd 4: *2 sc in next st, sc in next 2 sts* 6 times (24 sts).

Sl st in next st. Fasten off with long tail.

BEAK

With yellow yarn, ch 7.

Row 1: starting in 2nd ch from hook, sc2tog, sc in next 2 sts, sc2tog (4 sts).

Row 2: ch 1, turn, sc2tog, sc2tog (2 sts).

Row 3: ch 1, turn, sc2tog (1 st).

Fasten off with long tail.

EAR (MAKE 2)

Cut two 6-inch strands of pink yarn and two 6-inch strands of turquoise yarn. Lay strands together and attach to side of Head using Fringe technique (see page 13). Trim to 1 inch. Repeat on other side of Head.

ASSEMBLY

Sew Inner Eyes to Outer Eyes. Sew Eyes and Beak to Head. Weave in ends. ♦

Whoo!

Whoo!

Whoo!

Busy Bee

SUPPLIES

Worsted weight yarn in yellow (approx. 75 yards), black (approx. 25 yards) and small amount of white

Size H/8 (5 mm) crochet hook

Toilet paper roll

2 black animal eyes, 18 mm (optional)

Disappearing ink marking pen

Hole punch

Stitch marker

Yarn needle

HEAD AND BODY

Make Basic Roll Cover (see page 17) using yellow yarn for Top and Rnds 1-6 of Sides, then alternate 2 rnds of black with 2 rnds of yellow for the remainder.

EYE (MAKE 2)

Use animal eyes or crochet as follows.

With black yarn, make a magic ring, ch 1.

Rnd 1: 6 sc in ring, pull ring closed tight (6 sts).

Sl st in next st. Fasten off with long tail.

ANTENNA (MAKE 2)

With black yarn, make a magic ring, ch 1.

Rnd 1: 6 sc in ring, pull ring closed tight (6 sts).

Rnd 2: sc in each st around.

Rnd 3: *sc in next st, sc2tog* 2 times (4 sts).

Rnds 4-?: sc in each st around until antenna measures 2" long. Fasten off with long tail. Thread yarn needle with long tail and run yarn up and down through length of antenna 2 times to stiffen.

WING (MAKE 2)

With white yarn, make a magic ring, ch 1.

Rnd 1: 6 sc in ring, pull ring closed tight (6 sts).

Rnd 2: 2 sc in each st around. Place marker for beginning of rnd and move marker up as each rnd is completed. (12 sts).

Rnd 3: *sc in next st, 2 sc in next st* 6 times (18 sts).

Rnds 4-10: sc in each st around.

Fasten off with long tail.

MOUTH

To mark mouth, trace template onto office paper (see page 89). Punch holes in curve at intervals. Place template in position and dot with disappearing ink into the holes. Remove paper and connect the dots.

With black yarn, sew along outline with running stitch. Now sew in opposite direction to fill in the spaces, inserting needle through a bit of the stitches on either side to avoid gaps.

ASSEMBLY

Attach Eyes to face. If safety eyes are used, clip off excess stem with wire cutters. Sew Antennae to top of Head and Wings to top of Body. Weave in ends. ♦

Monty Monster

SUPPLIES

Worsted weight yarn in blue (approx. 100 yards) plus small amount of orange, yellow, red, white and black

Size H/8 (5 mm) crochet hook

Toilet paper roll

2 black buttons, 5/8" diameter (optional)

Fiberfill stuffing

Stitch marker

Yarn needle

Tooth Guide

HEAD

Make Basic Roll Cover (see page 17) using blue yarn.

OUTER EYE (MAKE 2)

With yellow yarn, make a magic ring, ch 1.

Rnd 1: 8 sc in ring, pull ring closed tight (8 sts).

Rnd 2a: 2 sc in next 3 sts (6 sts).

Point: ch 2 and sc in 2nd ch from hook, sc in next st.

Rnd 2b: 2 sc in next 3 sts (6 sts).

Point: ch 2 and sc in 2nd ch from hook, sc in next st.

Sl st in next st. Fasten off with long tail.

INNER EYE (MAKE 2)

Use buttons or crochet as follows.

With black yarn, make a magic ring, ch 1.

Rnd 1: 6 sc in ring, pull ring closed tight.

Sl st in next st. Fasten off with long tail.

MOUTH

With red yarn, ch 14 loosely.

Row 1: sc in 2nd ch from hook and in each remaining ch across (13 sts).

Rows 2-4: ch 1, turn, sc in each st across (13 sts).

Fasten off with long tail.

TOOTH (MAKE 12)

With white yarn, embroider 6 pointy teeth across top and bottom of mouth making each tooth about 1/2" x 1/2" and wrapping sts around edge of mouth: Referring to Tooth Guide above, bring needle up at A, wrap around edge at B, up at A, wrap around edge at C, etc. to create a triangle. Weave in ends.

HORN (MAKE 2)

With orange yarn, make a magic ring, ch 1.

Rnd 1: 4 sc in ring, pull ring closed tight (4 sts).

Rnd 2: *sc in next st, 2 sc in next st* 2 times. Place marker for beginning of rnd and move marker up as each rnd is completed (6 sts).

Rnd 3: sc in each st around.

Rnd 4: *sc in next 2 sts, 2 sc in next st* 2 times (8 sts).

Rnd 5: sc in next st, sl st in next 2 sts, sc in next 5 sts (8 sts).

Rnd 6: sc in next st, sl st in next 2 sts, 2 sc in next st, sc in next 3 sts, 2 sc in next st (10 sts).

Rnd 7: sc in next st, sl st in next 2 sts, sc in next 7 sts (10 sts).

Rnd 8: *sc in next 4 sts, 2 sc in next st* 2 times (12 sts).

Rnd 9: sc in each st around.

Rnd 10: *sc in next 5 sts, 2 sc in next st* 2 times (14 sts).

Rnd 11: sc in each st around.

Rnd 12: *sc in next 6 sts, 2 sc in next st* 2 times (16 sts).

Sl st in next st. Fasten off with long tail.

ASSEMBLY

Sew Inner Eyes to Outer Eyes and sew Eyes to Head. Sew Mouth in place. Stuff Horns and sew to top of Head. Weave in ends. ♦

Francesca & Frankie Frog

SUPPLIES

Worsted weight yarn in green (approx. 120 yards per frog) plus small amount of raspberry, pink and black

Size H/8 (5 mm) crochet hook

Toilet paper roll

Black animal eyes, 15 mm

Small piece of white craft foam

Fiberfill stuffing

Disappearing ink marking pen

Hole punch

Stitch marker

Yarn needle

HEAD

Make Basic Roll Cover (see page 17) using green yarn.

INNER EYE (MAKE 2)

Cut a circle of craft foam slightly larger than safety eye, about 3/4" diameter (see template below).

Cut an "x" in the center and insert stem of safety eye.

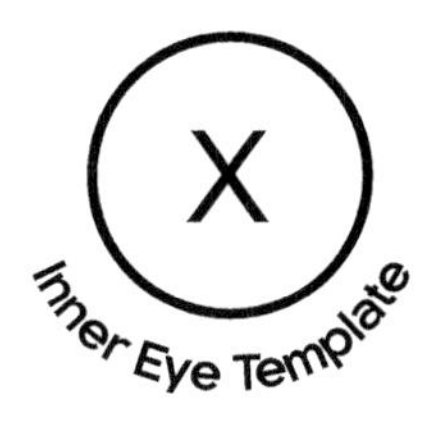

OUTER EYE (MAKE 2)

With green yarn, make a magic ring, ch 1.

Rnd 1: 6 sc in ring, pull ring closed tight (6 sts).

Rnd 2: 2 sc in each st around. Place marker for beginning of rnd and move marker up as each rnd is completed (12 sts).

Rnd 3: *sc in next st, 2 sc in next st* 6 times (18 sts).

Rnd 4: *sc in next 2 sts, 2 sc in next st* 6 times (24 sts).

Rnds 5-9: sc in each st around.

Fasten off with long tail.

BOW

With pink (Francesca) or black (Frankie) yarn, ch 6 loosely.

Row 1: sc in 2nd chain from hook and in each ch across (5 sts).

Rows 2-3: ch 1, turn, sc in eacl across (5 sts).

Rnd 4: sc in each st around n 3 sides. Join with sl st to next Fasten off.

Weave ends into wrong side. V a scrap of yarn, tie tightly acr center of rectangle. Wrap 1 e around center several times make a pretty pinched mid Knot ends together leaving l tails.

MOUTH

To mark mouth, trace template onto office paper (see page 89). Punch holes in tips. Place template in position and dot with disappearing ink into the holes. Remove paper and connect dots.

With raspberry yarn, sew along outline with running stitch. Now sew in opposite direction to fill in the spaces, inserting needle through a bit of the stitches on either side to avoid gaps.

ASSEMBLY

Attach Inner Eye to front of Outer Eye. Sew Bow to top of Eye for Francesca. Stuff Eyes with fiberfill and sew to top of Head. Sew Bow below Mouth for Frankie. Weave in ends. ♦

Leo Lion

SUPPLIES

Worsted weight yarn in golden-yellow (approx. 140 yards) and small amount of black plus variegated brown novelty or homespun yarn (approx. 15 yards)

Size H/8 (5 mm) crochet hook

Toilet paper roll

2 brown animal eyes, 15 mm

1 triangle animal nose, 21 mm

Disappearing ink marking pen

Small piece of cardboard

Fiberfill stuffing

Stitch marker

Yarn needle

HEAD AND BODY

Make Basic Roll Cover (see page 17) using golden-yellow yarn.

SNOUT

With golden-yellow yarn, make a magic ring, ch 1.

Rnd 1: 6 sc in ring, pull ring closed tight (6 sts).

Rnd 2: 2 sc in each st around. Place marker for beginning of rnd and move marker up as each rnd is completed (12 sts).

Rnd 3: *sc in next st, 2 sc in next st* 6 times (18 sts).

Rnd 4: *sc in next 2 sts, 2 sc in next st* 6 times (24 sts).

Rnd 5: *sc in next 3 sts, 2 sc in next st* 6 times (30 sts).

Rnds 6-7: sc in each st around.

Sl st in next st. Fasten off with long tail.

LEG (MAKE 4)

With golden-yellow yarn, make a magic ring, ch 1.

Rnd 1: 6 sc in ring, pull ring closed tight (6 sts).

Rnd 2: 2 sc in each st around. Place marker for beginning of rnd and move marker up as each rnd is completed (12 sts).

Rnd 3: *sc in next st, 2 sc in next st* 6 times (18 sts).

Rnds 4-8: sc in each st around.

Sl st in next st. Fasten off with long tail.

MANE

You will need many 4-inch pieces of variegated brown yarn to make the Mane. To quickly cut the 4-inch strands, wrap yarn widthwise around a 2" x 6" piece of cardboard. On one side, insert scissors between cardboard and yarn—and cut. Put Head and Body on toilet paper roll. Lay 2 strands together side-by-side. Put hook through a st on rib surrounding face and follow instructions for Fringe (see page 13). Continue making fringe in this manner around perimeter of face. Trim straggly ends.

TAIL

With golden-yellow yarn, make a chain about 2 1/2" long. Sc in 2nd chain from hook and in each ch across.

Fasten off with long tail. For tassel, pull two 4-inch strands of variegated brown yarn through end of tail using Fringe technique (see page 13).

ASSEMBLY

With black yarn, embroider straight stitch mouth (see diagram below) on Snout. Attach nose to Snout—just below center, between 2nd and 3rd ribs. Stuff Snout, pull gently at top and bottom to make a slightly oval shape, and sew in place. Attach eyes, clipping off excess stem with wire cutters. Mark position of Legs with Leg Templates (see page 90). Stuff Legs and sew to Body. Tie Tail to Body. Weave in ends. ♦

Mouth

Chester Chicken

SUPPLIES

Worsted weight yarn in white (approx. 100 yards) plus small amount of red, yellow and black

Size H/8 (5 mm) crochet hook

Toilet paper roll

2 black buttons, 3/4" diameter (optional)

Small piece of cardboard

Stitch marker

Yarn needle

HEAD

Make Basic Roll Cover (see page 17) using white yarn.

COMB

Cut a rectangle of cardboard measuring 2" x 6". Wrap red yarn widthwise around the cardboard 75 times. Carefully slide yarn off cardboard. Using a scrap of yarn, tie bundle together tightly around the middle. Cut loops open. Fluff pom pom and trim ends into a nice round shape.

EYE (MAKE 2)

Use buttons or crochet as follows.

With black yarn, make a magic ring, ch 1.

Rnd 1: 6 sc in ring, pull ring closed tight (6 sts).

Sl st in next st. Fasten off with long tail.

BEAK (MAKE 2)

Crochet until Beak is 2 inches long. You may need to stop before Rnd 9 depending on the thickness of your yarn.

With yellow yarn, make a magic ring, ch 1.

Rnd 1: 4 sc in ring, pull ring closed tight (4 sts).

Rnd 2: sc in next 3 sts, 2 sc in next st. Place marker for beginning of rnd and move marker up as each rnd is completed (5 sts).

Rnd 3: sc in next 4 sts, 2 sc in next st (6 sts).

Rnd 4: sc in next 5 sts, 2 sc in next st (7 sts).

Rnd 5: sc in next 6 sts, 2 sc in next st (8 sts).

Rnd 6: sc in next 7 sts, 2 sc in next st (9 sts).

Rnd 7: sc in next 8 sts, 2 sc in next st (10 sts).

Rnd 8: sc in next 9 sts, 2 sc in next st (11 sts).

Rnd 9: sc in next 10 sts, 2 sc in next st (12 sts).

Fasten off with long tail.

ASSEMBLY

Flatten and stack Beak pieces. Sew the two adjoining edges together to make a hinge. Sew Beak and Eyes to front of Head. Tie Comb to top of Head. Weave in ends. ♦

CLUCK

CLUCK

CLUCK

Lucky Duck

SUPPLIES

Worsted weight yarn in yellow (approx. 100 yards) plus small amount of orange and white

Size H/8 (5 mm) crochet hook

Toilet paper roll

2 black buttons, 1/2" diameter

Sewing needle and thread

Stitch marker

Yarn needle

HEAD

Make Basic Roll Cover (see page 17) using yellow yarn

OUTER EYE (MAKE 2)

The eye is worked around a foundation chain.

With white yarn, ch 4 loosely.

Rnd 1: starting in 2nd ch from hook, *sc in next 2 sts, 3 sc in next st* 2 times (10 sts).

Sl st in next st. Fasten off with long tail.

BEAK

With orange yarn, make a magic ring, ch 1.

Rnd 1: 6 sc in ring, pull ring closed tight (6 sts).

Rnd 2: 2 sc in each st around. Place marker for beginning of rnd and move marker up as each rnd is completed (12 sts).

Rnd 3: *sc in next st, 2 sc in next st* 6 times (18 sts).

Rnd 4: *sc in next 2 sts, 2 sc in next st* 6 times (24 sts).

Rnd 5: *sc in next 3 sts, 2 sc in next st* 6 times (30 sts).

Rnd 6: *sc in next 4 sts, 2 sc in next st* 6 times (36 sts).

Fasten off with long tail.

TUFT

Cut four 6-inch strands of yellow yarn. Lay strands together side by side and attach to top of Head using Fringe technique (see page 13). Trim ends even.

ASSEMBLY

Fold Beak in half, wrong sides together. Make 2 whip stitches at each corner to hold the crease. Sew buttons off-center to Outer Eyes. Sew Eyes and Beak to Head. Weave in ends. ♦

Quack

Party Cake

SUPPLIES

Worsted weight yarn in light pink (approx. 100 yards) plus small amount of hot pink, green, white, blue and yellow

Size H/8 (5 mm) crochet hook

Toilet paper roll

Disappearing ink marking pen

Hole punch

Fiberfill stuffing

Stitch marker

Yarn needle

CAKE

Make Basic Roll Cover (see page 17) using light pink yarn.

FROSTING BORDER

With white yarn, fasten on at bottom of Cake.

Rnd 1: *5 sc in next st, skip 1 st, sl st in next st* around.

Fasten off.

UPPER SCALLOP (MAKE 6)

Look at top of Cake to identify 6 sides created by its hexagonal shape (see Figure A on page 36). Each section gets a Scallop.

To mark Scallops, trace template (see page 90) onto office paper. Punch holes in curve at intervals.

Place template in position and dot with disappearing ink into the holes. Remove paper and connect the dots.

Using hot pink yarn, embroider Scallops with chain stitch embroidery (see page 14).

LOWER SCALLOP (MAKE 6)

To mark Scallops, trace template (see page 90) onto office paper. Punch holes in curve at intervals. Place template in position and dot with disappearing ink into the holes. Remove paper and connect the dots.

Using green yarn, embroider Scallops with chain stitch embroidery (see page 14).

BAUBLE (MAKE 6)

With hot pink yarn, make a magic ring, ch 1.

Rnd 1: 6 sc in ring, pull ring closed tight (6 sts).

Rnd 2: 2 sc in each st around Place marker for beginning of rnd and move marker up as each rnd is completed (12 sts).

Rnds 3-4: sc in each st around.

Fasten off with long tail.

DOLLOP

With white yarn, make a magic ring, ch 1.

Rnd 1: 6 sc in ring, pull ring closed tight (6 sts).

Rnd 2: 2 sc in each st around. Place marker for beginning of rnd and move marker up as each rnd is completed (12 sts).

Rnd 3: *sc in next st, 2 sc in next st* 6 times (18 sts).

Rnd 4: *2 sc in next st, sc in next 2 sts* 6 times (24 sts).

Rnd 5: *5 sc in next st, skip 1 st, sl st in next st* around.

Sl st to next st. Fasten off with long tail.

CANDLE

With blue yarn, make a magic ring, ch 1.

Rnd 1: 6 sc in ring, pull ring closed tight (6 sts).

Rnd 2: 2 sc in each st around (12 sts).

Rnds 3-?: sc in each st around until piece measures 3" .

Fasten off with long tail.

FLAME

With yellow yarn, make a magic ring, ch 1.

Rnd 1: 4 sc in ring, pull ring closed tight (4 sts).

Rnd 2: sc in each st around.

Rnd 3: *sc in next st, 2 sc in next st* 2 times (6 sts).

Rnd 4: *sc in next 2 sts, 2 sc in next st* 2 times (8 sts).

Rnd 5: *sc in next 3 sts, 2 sc in next st* 2 times (10 sts).

Rnd 6: sc in each st around.

Rnd 7: *sc in next 3 sts, sc2tog* 2 times (8 sts).

Rnd 8: *sc in next 2 sts, sc2tog* 2 times (6 sts).

Fasten off with long tail. Push and pinch to sculpt piece into a pretty flame shape.

ASSEMBLY

Sew Dollop to top of Cake. Stuff Candle and sew Flame on top. Sew Candle to Cake. Stuff Baubles and sew on top of Scallops. Weave in ends. ♦

FIGURE A

Top View of Cake

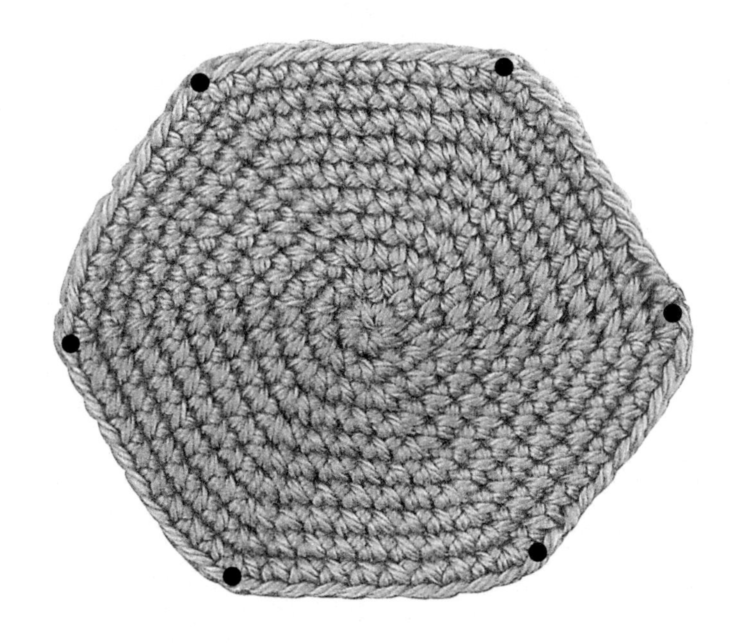

Mark Scallops between dots on sides of cake.

Alan the Alien

SUPPLIES

Worsted weight yarn in medium green (approx. 130 yards) plus small amount of light green and black

Size H/8 (5 mm) crochet hook

Toilet paper roll

2 brown animal eyes, 15 mm

Disappearing ink marking pen

Hole punch

Fiberfill stuffing

Stitch marker

Yarn needle

HEAD

Make Basic Roll Cover (see page 17) using medium green yarn.

OUTER EYE (MAKE 2)

With light green yarn, make a magic ring, ch 1.

Rnd 1: 6 sc in ring, pull ring closed almost tight, leaving room to insert post of eye (6 sts).

Rnd 2: 2 sc in each st around. Place marker for beginning of rnd and move marker up as each rnd is completed (12 sts).

Rnd 3: *sc in next st, 2 sc in next st* 6 times (18 sts).

Rnds 4-5: sc in each st around.

Fasten off with long tail.

EAR (MAKE 2)

With medium green yarn, make a magic ring, ch 1.

Rnd 1: 6 sc in ring, pull ring closed tight (6 sts).

Rnds 2-3: sc in each st around. Place marker for beginning of rnd and move marker up as each rnd is completed.

Rnd 4: *sc in next st, 2 sc in next st* 3 times (9 sts).

Rnds 5-6: sc in each st around.

Rnd 7: *sc in next 2 sts, 2 sc in next st* 3 times (12 sts).

Rnds 8-9: sc in each st around.

Rnd 10: *sc in next 3 sts, 2 sc in next st* 3 times (15 sts).

Rnd 11: sc in each st around.

Note: Change to working in rows.

Row 12: sc in next 8 sts (8 sts).

Row 13: ch 1, turn, sc2tog, sc in next 4 sts, sc2tog (6 sts).

Row 14: ch 1, turn, sc2tog, sc in next 2 sts, sc2tog (4 sts).

Row 15: ch 1, turn, sc2tog, sc2tog (2 sts).

Fasten off with long tail.

ANTENNA

With medium green yarn, make a magic ring, ch 1.

Rnd 1: 4 sc in ring, pull ring closed tight (4 sts).

Rnd 2: *sc in next st, 2 sc in next st* 2 times. Place marker for beginning of rnd and move marker up as each rnd is completed (6 sts).

Rnd 3: sc in each st around.

Rnd 4: *sc in next 2 sts, 2 sc in next st* 2 times (8 sts).

Rnd 5: sc in each st around.

Rnd 6: *sc in next 3 sts, 2 sc in next st* 2 times (10 sts).

Rnd 7: sc in each st around.

Rnd 8: *sc in next 4 sts, 2 sc in next st* 2 times (12 sts).

Rnd 9: sc in each st around.

Rnd 10: *sc in next 5 sts, 2 sc in next st* 2 times (14 sts).

Rnd 11: sc in each st around.

Rnd 12: *sc in next 6 sts, 2 sc in next st* 2 times (16 sts).

Rnd 13: sc in each st around.

Rnd 14: *sc in next 7 sts, 2 sc in next st* 2 times (18 sts).

Sl st in next st. Fasten off with long tail.

MOUTH

To mark mouth, trace template *(see page 91)* *onto office paper. Punch holes in curve at intervals. Place template in position and dot with disappearing ink into the holes. Remove paper and connect the dots.*

With black yarn, sew along outline with running stitch. Now sew in opposite direction to fill in the spaces, inserting needle through

ASSEMBLY

Attach animal eyes to center of Outer Eyes. Stuff Eyes and Antenna and sew to Head. Sew Ears to Head. Weave in ends. ♦

Jack O'Lantern

SUPPLIES

Worsted weight yarn in orange (approx. 100 yards) plus small amount of green and black

Size H/8 (5 mm) crochet hook

Toilet paper roll

Fiberfill stuffing

Disappearing ink marking pen

Hole punch

Stitch marker

Yarn needle

PUMPKIN

Make Basic Roll Cover (see page 17) using orange yarn.

STEM

With green yarn, make a magic ring, ch 1.

Rnd 1: 4 sc in ring, pull ring closed tight (4 sts).

Rnd 2: *sc in next st, 2 sc in next st* 2 times (6 sts).

Rnd 3: sc in each st around.

Rnd 4: *sc in next 2 sts, 2 sc in next st* 2 times (8 sts).

Rnd 5: sc in next st, sl st in next 2 sts, sc in next 5 sts (8 sts).

Rnd 6: sc in next st, sl st in the next 2 sts, 2 sc in next st, sc in next 3 sts, 2 sc in next st (10 sts).

Rnd 7: sc in next st, sl st in next 2 sts, sc in the next 7 sts (10 sts).

Rnd 8: *sc in next 4 sts, 2 sc in next st* 2 times (12 sts).

Rnd 9: sc in each st around.

Rnd 10: *sc in next 5 sts, 2 sc in next st* 2 times (14 sts).

Rnd 11: sc in each st around.

Rnd 12: *sc in next 6 sts, 2 sc in next st* 2 times (16 sts).

Sl st in next st. Fasten off with long tail.

LEAF

With green yarn, make a magic ring, ch 1.

Rnd 1: 8 sc in ring, pull ring closed tight (8 sts).

Rnd 2: 2 sc in each st around (16 sts).

Rnd 3: *5 sc in next st, skip 1 st, sl st in next st * around.

Fasten off with long tail.

TENDRIL

With green yarn, ch 25 loosely.

Row 1: sc in 2nd ch from hook and in each ch across (24 sts).

Fasten off with long tail. Tie loose ends together. Curl with fingers into a twirl.

EYE (MAKE 2)

With black yarn, ch 5.

Row 1: starting in 2nd ch from hook, sc in each st across (4 sts).

Row 2: ch 1, turn, sc2tog twice (2 sts).

Row 3: ch 1, turn, sc in each st across (2 sts).

Row 4: ch 1, turn, sc2tog (1 st).

Fasten off with long tail. Weave tail in and out around sides to make sharp edges and weave tail through center to fill in any gaps. Pinch tips into sharp points.

MOUTH

To mark mouth, trace template onto office paper (see page 91). Punch holes in tips. Place in position and dot with disappearing ink into the holes. Remove paper and connect the dots.

With black yarn, sew along outline with running stitch. Now sew in opposite direction to fill in the spaces, inserting needle through a bit of the stitches on either side to avoid gaps.

ASSEMBLY

Sew Eyes to Pumpkin. Stuff Stem and sew to top of Pumpkin. Sew Leaf and Tendril against Stem. Weave in ends. ♦

California Roll Sushi

SUPPLIES

Worsted weight yarn in black (approx. 75 yards) and white (approx 25 yards) plus small amount of orange, light green and medium green

Size H/8 (5 mm) crochet hook

Toilet paper roll

Stitch marker

Yarn needle

SUSHI ROLL

Make Basic Roll Cover (see page 17) using white yarn for Top and black yarn for Sides.

CRAB

With orange yarn, separate 1 ply from an 8 foot length. Hold the single orange ply together with white yarn and make a long chain of about 100 sts. Fasten off with long tail.

AVOCADO

With green yarn, ch 13 loosely.

Row 1: sc in 2nd ch from hook and in each st across (12 sts).

Row 2: ch 1, turn, sc in each st across (12 sts).

Row 3: ch 1, turn, sc2tog, sc in next 8 sts, sc2tog (10 sts).

Fasten off with long tail.

CUCUMBER

With light green yarn, ch 11 loosely.

Row 1: sc in 2nd ch from hook and in each st across (10 sts).

Row 2: ch 1, turn, sc in each st across (10 sts).

Fasten off with long tail.

CARROT

With orange yarn, ch 9.

Row 1: starting in 2nd ch from hook, sc2tog, sc in next 4 sts, sc2tog (6 sts).

Row 2: ch 1, turn, sc2tog, sc in next 2 sts, sc2tog (4 sts).

Row 3: ch 1, turn, sc2tog, sc2tog (2 sts).

Row 4: ch 1, turn, sc2tog (1 st).

Fasten off with long tail.

ASSEMBLY

With black yarn, sew an outline in groove between 6th and 7th ribs of Top: sew with running stitch, turn and sew in opposite direction filling in the gaps. Pile Crab into a mound. Fit all fillings into black outline and sew in place. Weave in ends. ♦

Oscar Octopus

SUPPLIES

Worsted weight yarn in lavender (approx. 300 yards) plus small amount of white and black

Size H/8 (5 mm) crochet hook

Toilet paper roll

2 black animal eyes, 18 mm (optional)

One 9"x12" sheet of white craft foam

1/4" hole punch

Sewing needle and lavender thread

Stitch marker

Yarn needle

HEAD

Make Basic Roll Cover (see page 17) using lavender yarn.

INNER EYE (MAKE 2)

Use animal eyes or crochet as follows.

With black yarn, make a magic ring, ch 1.

Rnd 1: 6 sc in ring, pull ring closed tight (6 sts).

Sl st in next st. Fasten off with long tail.

OUTER EYE (MAKE 2)

With white yarn, make a magic ring, ch 1.

Rnd 1: 6 sc in ring, pull ring closed almost tight (6 sts).

Rnd 2: 2 sc in each st around. Place marker for beginning of rnd and move marker up as each rnd is completed (12 sts).

Rnd 3: *sc in next st, 2 sc in next st* 6 times (18 sts).

Rnds 4-5: sc in each st around.

Fasten off with long tail.

ARM (MAKE 8)

With lavender yarn, make a magic ring, ch 1.

Rnd 1: 6 sc in ring, pull ring closed tight (6 sts).

Rnds 2-5: sc in each st around. Place marker for beginning of rnd and move marker up as each rnd is completed.

Rnd 6: *sc in next 2 sts, 2 sc in next st* 2 times (8 sts).

Rnds 7-15: sc in each st around.

Rnd 16: *sc in next 3 sts, 2 sc in next st* 2 times (10 sts).

Rnds 17-25: sc in each st around.

Rnd 26: *sc in next 4 sts, 2 sc in next st* 2 times (12 sts).

Rnds 27-39: sc in each st around.

Flatten open end and sc edges together. Fasten off with long tail.

SUCTION CUPS

Punch 1/4" circles of craft foam. With needle and thread, attach circles to underside of arms by embroidering a French knot at center: place 1 circle at tip and 2 circles across alternate ribs for remaining length of arm.

ASSEMBLY

Sew Arms at equal intervals to lower edge of Head. Attach Inner Eye to center of Outer Eye. Stuff Eyes and sew to Head. Coil Arms in different directions and sew to secure position, if desired. Weave in ends. ♦

Snowman Sam

SUPPLIES

Worsted weight yarn in white (approx. 150 yards) and black (approx 55 yards) plus small amount of blue, orange and brown

Size H/8 (5 mm) crochet hook

Toilet paper roll

5 black buttons, 3/8" diameter

Sewing needle and thread

Disappearing ink marking pen

Hole punch

Fiberfill stuffing

Stitch marker

Yarn needle

BODY

Make Basic Roll Cover (see page 17) with white yarn.

HEAD

With white yarn, make a magic ring, ch 1.

Rnd 1: 6 sc in ring, pull ring closed tight (6 sts).

Rnd 2: 2 sc in each st around. Place marker for beginning of rnd and move marker up as each rnd is completed (12 sts).

Rnd 3: *sc in next st, 2 sc in next st* 6 times (18 sts).

Rnd 4: *sc in next 2 sts, 2 sc in next st* 6 times (24 sts).

Rnd 5: *sc in next 3 sts, 2 sc in next st* 6 times (30 sts).

Rnd 6: *sc in next 4 sts, 2 sc in next st* 6 times (36 sts).

Rnd 7: *sc in next 5 sts, 2 sc in next st* 6 times (42 sts).

Rnd 8: *sc in next 6 sts, 2 sc in next st* 6 times (48 sts).

Rnd 9: *sc in next 7 sts, 2 sc in next st* 6 times (54 sts).

Rnds 10-18: sc in each st around.

Rnd 19: *sc in next 7 sts, sc2tog* 6 times (48 sts).

Rnd 20: *sc in next 6 sts, sc2tog* 6 times (42 sts).

Rnd 21: *sc in next 5 sts, sc2tog* 6 times (36 sts).

Rnd 22: *sc in next 4 sts, sc2tog* 6 times (30 sts).

Rnd 23: *sc in next 3 sts, sc2tog* 6 times (24 sts).

Fasten off with long tail.

NOSE

With orange yarn, make a magic ring, ch 1.

Rnd 1: 5 sc in ring, pull ring closed tight (5 sts).

Rnds 2-3: sc in each st around. Place marker for beginning of rnd and move marker up as each rnd is completed

Rnd 4: 2 sc in next st, sc in next 2 sts, 2 sc in next st, sc in next st (7 sts).

Rnds 5-6: sc in each st around.

Sl st in next st. Fasten off with long tail.

ARM (MAKE 2)

To mark arm, trace template (see page 91) onto office paper. Punch holes in ends, wrist and elbow. Place template in position and dot with disappearing ink into the holes. Remove paper and connect the dots.

With brown yarn, sew along outline with a running stitch. Now sew in opposite direction to fill in the spaces, inserting needle through a bit of the stitches on either side to avoid gaps.

SCARF

With blue yarn, ch 5 loosely.

Row 1: sc in 2nd ch from hook and in each st across (4 sts).

Rows 2-?: *ch 1, turn, sc in each st across* until scarf is 18" long (4 sts).

To make fringe, cut sixteen 4-inch

strands of yarn. Lay 2 strands together side-by-side. Put hook through 1st st on one end of scarf and follow Fringe instructions on page 13. Continue making fringe across both ends of scarf. Trim ends to be even.

HAT

With black yarn, make a magic ring, ch 1.

Rnd 1: 6 sc in ring, pull ring closed tight (6 sts).

Rnd 2: 2 sc in each st around. Place marker for beginning of rnd and move marker up as each rnd is completed (12 sts).

Rnd 3: *sc in next st, 2 sc in next st* 6 times (18 sts).

Rnd 4: *sc in next 2 sts, 2 sc in next st* 6 times (24 sts).

Rnd 5: *sc in next 3 sts, 2 sc in next st* 6 times (30 sts).

Rnd 6: *sc in next 4 sts, 2 sc in next st* 6 times (36 sts).

Rnd 7: *sc in next 5 sts, 2 sc in next st* 6 times (42 sts).

Rnd 8: *sc in next 6 sts, 2 sc in next st* 6 times (48 sts).

Rnd 9: *sc in next 7 sts, 2 sc in next st* 6 times (54 sts).

Rnds 10-15: sc in each st around.

Rnd 16: *sc in next 7 sts, sc2tog* 6 times (48 sts).

Rnd 17: *sc in next 6 sts, sc2tog* 6 times (42 sts).

Rnd 18: sc in each st around.

Rnd 19: *sc in next 2 sts, 2 sc in next st* 14 times (56 sts).

Rnd 20: *sc in next 2 sts, 2 sc in next st* 18 times, sc in next 2 sts (74 sts).

Rnds 21-23: sc in each st around.

Rnd 24: sl st in each st around.

Fasten off.

ASSEMBLY

On 10th rib of Head, mark 2 dots, 2" apart. Sew a button over each dot. Stuff Head. Mark dots around 7th rib of Basic Roll Cover for head position. Sew Head in place, pausing when nearly done to pack in more stuffing. Stuff Nose lightly and sew to Head. Sew 3 buttons down front of Body. Tie Scarf around neck and put Hat on Head. Weave in ends. ♦

Kitty Cat

SUPPLIES

Worsted weight yarn in gray (approx. 155 yards) plus small amount of white, pink and black

Size H/8 (5 mm) crochet hook

Toilet paper roll

2 green cat eyes, 18 mm

Fiberfill stuffing

Wooden spoon

Stitch marker

Yarn needle

HEAD AND BODY

Make Basic Roll Cover (see page 17) using gray yarn.

EAR (MAKE 2)

Make 1 ear piece with pink yarn and 1 ear piece with gray yarn.

With pink or gray yarn, chain 7 loosely.

Row 1: sc in 2nd chain from hook and each ch across (6 sts).

Rows 2-3: ch 1, turn, sc in each st across (6 sts).

Row 4: ch 1, turn, sc2tog, sc in next 2 sts, sc2tog (4 sts).

Row 5: ch 1, turn, sc in each st across (4 sts).

Row 6: ch 1, turn, sc2tog twice (2 sts).

Row 7: ch 1, turn, sc in each st across (2 sts).

Row 8: ch 1, turn, sc2tog (1 st).

Fasten off. Weave in ends, weaving over any holes made by decreases.

Place pink and gray pieces wrong sides together. With gray yarn, sc pieces together along outer edge making 3 sts at each corner. Fasten off with long tail.

LEG (MAKE 4)

With white yarn, make a magic ring, ch 1.

Rnd 1: 6 sc in ring, pull ring closed tight (6 sts).

Rnd 2: 2 sc in each st around. Place marker for beginning of rnd and move marker up as each rnd is completed (12 sts).

Rnd 3: *sc in next st, 2 sc in next st* 6 times (18 sts).

Rnds 4-5: sc in each st around; change to gray yarn in last st.

Rnds 6-8: sc in each st around.

Sl st in next st. Fasten off with long tail.

NOSE

With pink yarn, make a magic ring, ch 1.

Rnd 1: 4 sc in ring, pull ring closed tight (4 sts).

Sl st in next st. Fasten off with long tail.

SNOUT

With white yarn, make a magic ring, ch 1.

Rnd 1: 6 sc in ring, pull ring closed tight (6 sts).

Rnd 2: 2 sc in each st around. Place marker for beginning of rnd and move marker up as each rnd is completed (12 sts).

Rnd 3: *sc in next st, 2 sc in next st* 6 times (18 sts).

Rnd 4: *2 sc in next st, sc in next 2 sts* 6 times (24 sts).

Sl st in next st. Fasten off with long tail.

TAIL

With gray yarn, make a magic ring, ch 1.

Rnd 1: 5 sc in ring, pull ring closed tight (5 sts).

Rnd 2: 2 sc in each st around (10 sts).

Rnds 3-?: sc in each st around until tail is 4" long.

Sl st in next st. Fasten off with long tail.

ASSEMBLY

Sew Ears to Head. Sew Nose to Snout. With pink yarn, embroider straight stitch mouth (see diagram) on Snout. Pull left and right sides of Snout gently to make a slight oval and sew to face. With black yarn, embroider whiskers by making 1 long stitch for each whisker. Attach eyes, clipping off excess stem with wire cutters. Mark position of Legs with Leg Templates (see page 90). Stuff Legs and sew to Body. Stuff Tail using wooden spoon handle to push fiberfill into the tube. Sew Tail to Body. Weave in ends. ♦

Mouth

Rodney Robot

SUPPLIES

Worsted weight yarn in red (approx. 100 yards) plus small amount of white, black, gray and yellow

Size H/8 (5 mm) crochet hook

Toilet paper roll

2 black buttons, 1" diameter (optional)

Fiberfill stuffing

Stitch marker

Yarn needle

HEAD

Make Basic Roll Cover (see page 17) using red yarn.

INNER EYE (MAKE 2)

Use buttons or crochet as follows.

With black yarn, make a magic ring, ch 1.

Rnd 1: 6 sc in ring, pull ring closed tight (6 sts).

Rnd 2: 2 sc in each st around (12 sts).

Sl st in next st. Fasten off with long tail.

OUTER EYE (MAKE 2)

With white yarn, make a magic ring, ch 1.

Rnd 1: 6 sc in ring, pull ring closed tight (6 sts).

Rnd 2: 2 sc in each st around. Place marker for beginning of rnd and move marker up as each rnd is completed (12 sts).

Rnd 3: *sc in next st, 2 sc in next st* 6 times (18 sts).

Rnd 4: *2 sc in next st, sc in next 2 sts* 6 times (24 sts).

Sl st in next st. Fasten off with long tail.

LIGHT

Light is worked in back loops only.

With yellow yarn, make a magic ring, ch 1.

Rnd 1: 6 sc in ring, pull ring closed tight (6 sts).

Rnd 2: 2 sc in each st around. Place marker for beginning of rnd and move marker up as each rnd is completed (12 sts).

Rnd 3: *sc in next st, 2 sc in next st* 6 times (18 sts).

Rnd 4: *2 sc in next st, sc in next 2 sts* 6 times (24 sts).

Rnd 5: *sc in next 3 sts, 2 sc in next st* 6 times (30 sts).

Rnds 6-10: sc in each st around.

Fasten off with long tail.

BOLT (MAKE 2)

Bolt is worked in back loops only.

With gray yarn, make a magic ring, ch 1.

Rnd 1: 6 sc in ring, pull ring closed tight (6 sts).

Rnd 2: 2 sc in each st around. Place marker for beginning of rnd and move marker up as each rnd is completed (12 sts).

Rnd 3: *sc in next st, 2 sc in next st* 6 times (18 sts).

Rnd 4: *2 sc in next st, sc in next 2 sts* 6 times (24 sts).

Rnds 5-7: sc in each st around.

Fasten off with long tail.

MOUTH

With black yarn, ch 11 sts loosely.

Row 1: sc in 2nd ch from hook and in each ch across (10 sts).

Fasten off with long tail. Tie ends together.

ASSEMBLY

Stuff Light and sew to top of Head. Stuff Bolts and sew to sides of Head. Sew Inner Eyes to Outer Eyes. Sew Eyes and Mouth to head. Weave in ends. ♦

Monogram Mug

SUPPLIES

Worsted weight yarn in blue (approx. 135 yards) and brown (approx. 25 yards) plus small amount of white

Size H/8 (5 mm) crochet hook

Toilet paper roll

Disappearing ink marking pen

Hole punch (optional)

Wooden spoon

Stitch marker

Yarn needle

MUG

Make Basic Roll Cover (see page 17) using blue yarn and working Rnd 1 of Sides in back loops only. Resume working in both loops for remainder of Sides.

RIM

With blue yarn, fasten on at Rnd 1 of Sides where front loops were left unworked.

Rnd 1: ch 1, sc in each unworked front loop around.

Rnds 2-3: sc in each st around. Place marker for beginning of rnd and move marker up as each rnd is completed

Fasten off.

HANDLE

With blue yarn, make a magic ring, ch 1.

Rnd 1: 10 sc in ring, pull ring closed tight (10 sts).

Rnds 2-?: sc in each st around until tube measures 6" long.

Fasten off with long tail.

LIQUID

With brown yarn, follow instructions for Top of Basic Roll Cover.

Fasten off with long tail.

MONOGRAM

With disappearing ink marking pen, draw capital letter at center front of Mug. Using white yarn, embroider letter with chain stitch embroidery (see page 14).

Note: To mark a nice monogram, print a 2½" letter onto paper from a computer. Punch holes in letter at intervals. Place letter in position and dot with disappearing ink into the holes. Remove paper and connect dots.

ASSEMBLY

Stuff Handle using a wooden spoon handle to push fiberfill into the tube. Sew Handle to Mug with open end at top. Sew Liquid to top of Mug. Weave in ends. ♦

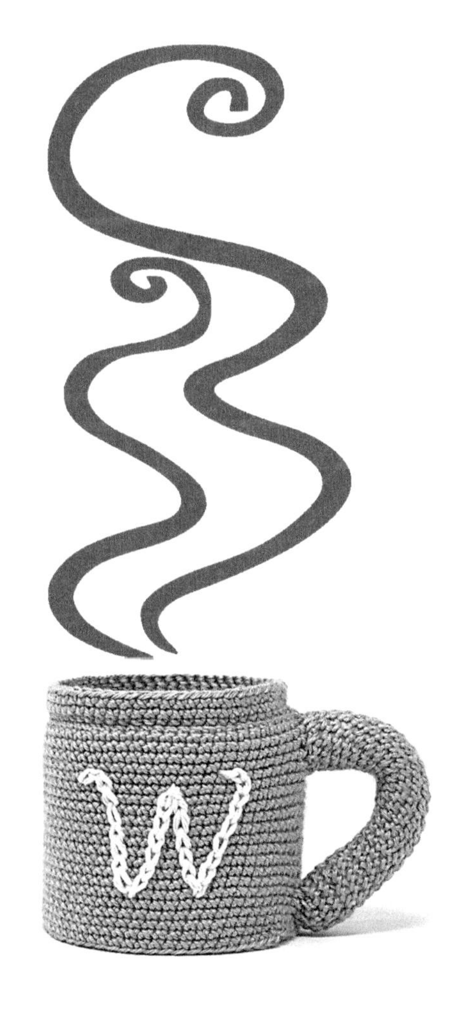

Peggy Pig

SUPPLIES

Worsted weight yarn in peach (approx. 170 yards) and small amount of black

Size H/8 (5 mm) crochet hook

Toilet paper roll

2 black buttons, 1/2" diameter (optional)

Fiberfill stuffing

Stitch marker

Yarn needle

HEAD AND BODY

Make Basic Roll Cover (see page 17) using peach yarn.

EYE (MAKE 2)

Use buttons or crochet as follows.

With black yarn, make a magic ring, ch 1.

Rnd 1: 6 sc in ring, pull ring closed tight (6 sts).

Sl st in next st. Fasten off with long tail.

EAR (MAKE 2)

With peach yarn, make a magic ring, ch 1.

Rnd 1: 6 sc in ring, pull ring closed tight (6 sts).

Rnd 2: *sc in next 2 sts, 2 sc in next st* 2 times. Place marker for beginning of rnd and move marker up as each rnd is completed (8 sts).

Rnd 3: *sc in next 3 sts, 2 sc in next st* 2 times (10 sts).

Rnd 4: *sc in next 4 sts, 2 sc in next st* 2 times (12 sts).

Rnd 5: *sc in next 5 sts, 2 sc in next st* 2 times (14 sts).

Rnd 6: *sc in next 6 sts, 2 sc in next st* 2 times (16 sts).

Rnd 7: *sc in next 7 sts, 2 sc in next st* 2 times (18 sts).

Rnd 8: *sc in next 8 sts, 2 sc in next st* 2 times (20 sts).

Rnds 9-10: sc in each st around.

Sl st in next st. Fasten off with long tail.

SNOUT

With peach yarn, make a magic ring, ch 1.

Rnd 1: 6 sc in ring, pull ring closed tight (6 sts).

Rnd 2: 2 sc in each st around. Place marker for beginning of rnd and move marker up as each rnd is completed (12 sts).

Rnd 3: *sc in next st, 2 sc in next st* 6 times (18 sts).

Rnd 4: *sc in next 2 sts, 2 sc in next st* 6 times (24 sts).

Rnds 5-8: sc in each st around.

Sl st in next st. Fasten off with long tail. With a double strand of black yarn, embroider 2 French knots for nostrils.

LEG (MAKE 4)

With peach yarn, make a magic ring, ch 1.

Rnd 1: 6 sc in ring, pull ring closed tight (6 sts).

Rnd 2: 2 sc in each st around. Place marker for beginning of rnd and move marker up as each rnd is completed (12 sts).

Rnd 3: *sc in next st, 2 sc in next st* 6 times (18 sts).

Rnds 4-8: sc in each st around.

Sl st in next st. Fasten off with long tail.

TAIL

With peach yarn, ch 11 loosely.

Row 1: 3 sc in 2nd ch from hook and in each ch across (30 sts).

Fasten off with long tail.

ASSEMBLY

Stuff Snout and sew slightly below center of face. Shape Ears into a slight curve and sew to Head. Mark position of Legs with Leg Templates (see page 90). Stuff Legs and sew to Body. Tie Tail to Body. Sew Eyes to face. Weave in ends. ♦

Simon Cow

SUPPLIES

Worsted weight yarn in white (approx. 120 yards) and black (approx. 55 yards) plus small amount of brown, light pink and dark pink

Size H/8 (5 mm) crochet hook

Toilet paper roll

Brown animal eyes, 15 mm

Fiberfill stuffing

Stitch marker

Yarn needle

HEAD AND BODY

Make Basic Roll Cover (see page 17) with white yarn.

SNOUT

The Snout is worked around a foundation chain.

With pink yarn, ch 8 loosely.

Rnd 1: starting in 2nd ch from hook, *sc in next 6 sts, 3 sc in next st* 2 times. Place marker for beginning of rnd and move marker up as each rnd is completed (18 sts).

Rnd 2: *sc in next 6 sts, 2 sc in next 3 sts* 2 times (24 sts).

Rnds 3-5: sc in each st around.

Sl st in next st. Fasten off with long tail.

EAR (MAKE 2)

With black yarn, make a magic ring, ch 1.

Rnd 1: 6 sc in ring, pull ring closed tight (6 sts).

Rnd 2: *sc in next 2 sts, 2 sc in next st* 2 times. Place marker for beginning of rnd and move marker up as each rnd is completed (8 sts).

Rnd 3: *sc in next 3 sts, 2 sc in next st" 2 times (10 sts).

Rnd 4: *sc in next 4 sts, 2 sc in next st" 2 times (12 sts).

Rnd 5: *sc in next 5 sts, 2 sc in next st" 2 times (14 sts).

Rnd 6: *sc in next 6 sts, 2 sc in next st" 2 times (16 sts).

Rnd 7: sc in each st around.

Rnd 8: *sc in next 6 sts, sc2tog* 2 times (14 sts).

Rnd 9: *sc in next 5 sts, sc2tog* 2 times (12 sts).

Rnd 10: *sc in next 4 sts, sc2tog* 2 times (10 sts).

Rnd 11: *sc in next 3 sts, sc2tog* 2 times (8 sts).

Sl st in next st. Fasten off with long tail.

SPOT (MAKE 3)

Each Spot is made in 2 sections.

Part A

With black yarn, make a magic ring, ch 1.

Rnd 1: 6 sc in ring, pull ring closed tight (6 sts).

Rnd 2: 2 sc in each st around. Place marker for beginning of rnd and move marker up as each rnd is completed (12 sts).

Rnd 3: *sc in next st, 2 sc in next st* 6 times (18 sts).

Rnd 4: *2 sc in next st, sc in next 2 sts* 6 times (24 sts).

Rnd 5: *sc in next 3 sts, 2 sc in next st* 6 times (30 sts).

Sl st in next st. Fasten off with long tail.

Part B

With black yarn, ch 2.

Row 1: 3 sc in 2nd ch from hook (3 sts).

Row 2: ch 1, turn, 2 sc in each st across (6 sts).

Row 3: ch 1, turn, *sc in next st, 2 sc in next st* 3 times (9 sts).

Row 4: ch 1, turn, *sc in next 2 sts, 2 sc in next st* 3 times (12 sts).

Fasten off with long tail. Place straight side of Part B anywhere against side of Part A and sew together.

HORN (MAKE 2)

With brown yarn, make a magic ring, ch 1.

Rnd 1: 4 sc in ring, pull ring closed tight (4 sts).

Rnd 2: sc in next 3 sts, 2 sc in next st. Place marker for beginning of rnd and move marker up as each rnd is completed (5 sts).

Rnd 3: sc in next 4 sts, 2 sc in next st (6 sts).

Rnd 4: sc in next 5 sts, 2 sc in next st (7 sts).

Rnd 5: sc in next 6 sts, 2 sc in next st (8 sts).

Fasten off with long tail.

LEG (MAKE 4)

With black yarn, make a magic ring, ch 1.

Rnd 1: 6 sc in ring, pull ring closed tight (6 sts).

Rnd 2: 2 sc in each st around. Place marker for beginning of rnd and move marker up as each rnd is completed (12 sts).

Rnd 3: *sc in next st, 2 sc in next st* 6 times (18 sts).

Rnd 4: sc in each st around; change to white yarn in last st.

Rnds 5-8: sc in each st around.

Sl st in next st. Fasten off with long tail.

TAIL

With white yarn, make a chain about 2 1/2" long. Sc in 2nd chain from hook and in each ch across.

Fasten off with long tail.

For tassel, cut two 4-inch strands of black yarn and attach to end of tail using technique for Fringe (see page 13). Trim ends.

ASSEMBLY

Attach eyes to face, clipping off excess stem with wire cutters. Sew Spots to Body—1 on each side and 1 on top. With a double strand of dark pink yarn, embroider 2 French knots on Snout. Stuff Snout and sew to lower half of face. Sew Ears and Horns to Body. Mark position of Legs with Leg Templates (see page 90). Stuff Legs and sew to Body. Tie Tail to Body. Weave in ends. ♦

Teddy Bear

SUPPLIES

Worsted weight yarn in tan (approx. 275 yards) plus small amount of red and aqua

Size H/8 (5 mm) crochet hook

Toilet paper roll

Fiberfill stuffing

Disappearing ink marking pen

2 brown animal eyes, 15 mm

1 triangle animal nose, 18 mm

Stitch marker

Yarn needle

BODY

Make Basic Roll Cover (see page 17) using tan yarn.

HEAD

Note: The thickness of your yarn can make a big difference to the size of the Head. To make your bear's Head larger or smaller, change your hook size up or down.

With tan yarn, make a magic ring, ch 1.

Rnd 1: 6 sc in ring, pull ring closed tight (6 sts).

Rnd 2: 2 sc in each st around. Place marker for beginning of rnd and move marker up as each rnd is completed (12 sts).

Rnd 3: *sc in next st, 2 sc in next st* 6 times (18 sts).

Rnd 4: *sc in next 2 sts, 2 sc in next st* 6 times (24 sts).

Rnd 5: *sc in next 3 sts, 2 sc in next st* 6 times (30 sts).

Rnd 6: *sc in next 4 sts, 2 sc in next st* 6 times (36 sts).

Rnd 7: *sc in next 5 sts, 2 sc in next st* 6 times (42 sts).

Rnd 8: *sc in next 6 sts, 2 sc in next st* 6 times (48 sts).

Rnd 9: *sc in next 7 sts, 2 sc in next st* 6 times (54 sts).

Rnd 10: *sc in next 8 sts, 2 sc in next st* 6 times (60 sts).

Rnds 11-20: sc in each st around.

Rnd 21: *sc in next 8 sts, sc2tog* 6 times (54 sts).

Rnd 22: *sc in next 7 sts, sc2tog* 6 times (48 sts).

Rnd 23: *sc in next 6 sts, sc2tog* 6 times (42 sts).

Rnd 24: *sc in next 5 sts, sc2tog* 6 times (36 sts).

Rnd 25: *sc in next 4 sts, sc2tog* 6 times (30 sts).

Rnd 26: *sc in next 3 sts, sc2tog* 6 times (24 sts).

Rnds 27-29: sc in each st around.

Fasten off with long tail.

SNOUT

With tan yarn, make a magic ring, ch 1.

Rnd 1: 6 sc in ring, pull ring closed tight (6 sts).

Rnd 2: 2 sc in each st around. Place marker for beginning of rnd and move marker up as each rnd is completed (12 sts).

Rnd 3: sc in each st around.

Rnd 4: *sc in next st, 2 sc in next st* 6 times (18 sts).

Rnd 5: sc in each st around.

Rnd 6: *sc in next 2 sts, 2 sc in next st* 6 times (24 sts).

Rnd 7: sc in each st around.

Sl st in next st. Fasten off with long tail.

EAR (MAKE 2)

With tan yarn, make a magic ring, ch 1.

Rnd 1: 6 sc in ring, pull ring closed tight (6 sts).

Rnd 2: 2 sc in each st around. Place marker for beginning of rnd and move marker up as each rnd is completed (12 sts).

Rnd 3: *sc in next st, 2 sc in next st* 6 times (18 sts).

Rnds 4-7: sc in each st around.

Fasten off with long tail.

ARM (MAKE 2)

With tan yarn, make a magic ring, ch 1.

Rnd 1: 6 sc in ring, pull ring closed tight (6 sts).

Rnd 2: 2 sc in each st around. Place marker for beginning of rnd and move marker up as each rnd is completed (12 sts).

Rnd 3: *sc in next st, 2 sc in next st* 6 times (18 sts).

Rnds 4-12: sc in each st around.

Fasten off with long tail.

LEG (MAKE 2)

With tan yarn, make a magic ring, ch 1.

Rnd 1: 6 sc in ring, pull ring closed tight (6 sts).

Rnd 2: 2 sc in each st around. Place marker for beginning of rnd and move marker up as each rnd is completed (12 sts).

Rnd 3: *sc in next st, 2 sc in next st* 6 times (18 sts).

Rnd 4: *sc in next 2 sts, 2 sc in next st* 6 times (24 sts).

Rnds 5-13: sc in each st around.

Fasten off with long tail.

TIE

With aqua yarn, ch 100 loosely.

Row 1: sc in 2nd ch from hook and in each remaining ch across (99 sts).

Rows 2-3: ch 1, turn, sc in each st across.

Fasten off. Weave in ends.

ASSEMBLY

Attach eyes 3" apart between Rnds 15 and 16 of Head. Flatten Ears and sew to top of Head. Attach nose slightly above center of Snout. With red yarn, embroider a straight stitch mouth. Stuff Snout and sew in place. Stuff Head, Arms and Legs. Place Body on roll of toilet paper to mark position of Head, Arms and Legs with disappearing ink marking pen: using templates (see page 92), mark Arm position even with top of roll and Leg position even with bottom of roll. Sew Head in place, then Arms and Legs. Weave in ends. Fasten Tie in a bow around neck. ♦

Sock Monkey

SUPPLIES

Worsted weight yarn in gray heather (approx. 50 yards) and off-white (approx. 45 yards) plus small amount of dark red and black

Size H/8 (5 mm) crochet hook

Toilet paper roll

2 black buttons, 3/4" diameter

Sewing needle and thread

Small piece of cardboard

Fiberfill stuffing

Stitch marker

Yarn needle

HEAD

Make Basic Roll Cover (see page 17) as follows: For the Top, use off-white yarn. For the Sides, use off-white yarn for Rnds 1-5, red yarn for Rnds 6-7 and gray yarn for the remainder.

SNOUT

The Snout is worked around a foundation chain.

With off-white yarn, ch 11 loosely.

Rnd 1: starting in 2nd ch from hook *sc in next 9 sts, 3 sc in next st* 2 times. Place marker for beginning of rnd and move marker up as each rnd is completed (24 sts).

Rnd 2: *sc in next 4 sts, 2 sc in next st, sc in next 4 sts, 2 sc in next 3 sts* 2 times (32 sts).

Rnds 3-5: sc in each st around.

Sl st in next st. Fasten off with long tail.

MOUTH

With red yarn, ch st until your work measures 3" long. Fasten off with long tail.

EAR (MAKE 2)

With gray yarn, make a magic ring, ch 1.

Rnd 1: 6 sc in ring, pull ring closed tight (6 sts).

Rnd 2: 2 sc in each st around. Place marker for beginning of rnd and move marker up as each rnd is completed (12 sts).

Rnd 3: *sc in next st, 2 sc in next st* 6 times (18 sts).

Rnd 4: sc in each st around.

Sl st in next st. Fasten off with long tail.

POM POM

Cut a rectangle of cardboard measuring 2" x 6". Wrap red yarn widthwise around cardboard 75 times. Carefully slide yarn off cardboard. Using a scrap of yarn, tie bundle together tightly around the middle. Cut loops open. Fluff pom pom and trim ends into a nice round shape.

ASSEMBLY

Sew Mouth in a curve to center of Snout. With black yarn, embroider 2 French knots to top of Snout. Stuff Snout and sew to Head. Sew button eyes and Ears to Head. Tie Pom Pom to top. Weave in ends. ♦

Bunny Rabbit

SUPPLIES

Worsted weight yarn in beige (approx. 125 yards) and small amount of pink

Size H/8 (5 mm) crochet hook

Toilet paper roll

2 black buttons, 1/2" diameter (optional)

Disappearing ink marking pen

Hole punch

Stitch marker

Yarn needle

HEAD

Make Basic Roll Cover (see page 17) with beige yarn.

EAR (MAKE 2)

With beige yarn, make a magic ring, ch 1.

Rnd 1: 6 sc in ring, pull ring closed tight (6 sts).

Rnd 2: 2 sc in each st around. Place marker for beginning of rnd and move marker up as each rnd is completed (12 sts).

Rnd 3: *sc in next st, 2 sc in next st* 6 times (18 sts).

Rnds 4-8: sc in each st around.

Rnd 9: *sc in next 4 sts, sc2tog* 3 times (15 sts).

Rnds 10-11: sc in each st around.

Rnd 12: *sc in next 3 sts, sc2tog* 3 times (12 sts).

Rnds 13-15: sc in each st around.

Fasten off with long tail. Sew open end together.

TAIL

Cut a rectangle of cardboard measuring 2" x 6". Wrap beige yarn widthwise around card-board 75 times. Carefully slide yarn off cardboard. Using a scrap of yarn, tie bundle together tightly around the middle. Cut loops open. Fluff pom pom and trim ends into a nice round shape.

EYE (MAKE 2)

Use buttons or crochet as follows.

With black yarn, make a magic ring, ch 1.

Rnd 1: 5 sc in ring, pull ring closed tight (5 sts).

Sl st in next st. Fasten off with long tail.

NOSE

With pink yarn, make a magic ring, ch 1.

Rnd 1: 4 sc in ring, pull ring closed tight (4 sts).

Sl st in next st. Fasten off with long tail.

MOUTH

To mark mouth, trace template onto office paper (see page 92). Punch holes in corners and tips. Place template in position and dot with disappearing ink into the holes. Remove paper and connect dots.

With pink yarn, sew along outline with running stitch. Now sew in opposite direction to fill in the spaces, inserting needle through a bit of the stitches on either side to avoid gaps.

TIE

With pink yarn, make a 17-inch chain.

Row 1: sc in 2nd chain from hook and in each remaining ch across.

Fasten off. Knot loose ends together. Weave in ends.

ASSEMBLY

Sew Nose, Eyes and Ears to Head. Fasten Tie in a bow around Ear. Tie Tail to lower back. Weave in ends. ♦

Flower Pot

SUPPLIES

Worsted weight yarn in brown (approx 120 yards), green (approx. 50 yards), purple (approx. 70 yards) and small amount of yellow

Size H/8 (5 mm) crochet hook

Toilet paper roll

Fiberfill stuffing

Stitch marker

Yarn needle

FLOWER POT

Make Basic Roll Cover (see page 17) using brown yarn.

TOPPER

Make according to instructions for Basic Roll Cover as follows: For the Top, use green yarn. For the Sides, use green yarn for Rnds 1-7; change to brown yarn in last st. For Rnds 8-14, continue with brown yarn. Fasten off with long tail.

FLOWER (MAKE 27)

With purple yarn, make a magic ring, ch 1.

Rnd 1: 5 sc in ring, pull ring closed tight (5 sts).

Rnd 2: 2 sc in each st around. Place marker for beginning of rnd and move marker up as each rnd is completed (10 sts).

Rnd 3: sc in each st around.

Rnd 4: 2 sc in each st around (20 sts).

Sl st in next st. Fasten off and weave in end. With a double strand of yellow yarn, embroider a French knot in center of flower. Knot loose ends.

ASSEMBLY

Sew Flowers to green area of Topper pulling all loose ends to the inside. Put Flower Pot on toilet paper roll: Stuff Topper with fiberfill and pin in place so that top of brown section aligns with top of toilet paper roll. Sew Topper in position. Weave in ends. ♦

Carl the Car

SUPPLIES

Worsted weight yarn in orange (approx. 140 yards) plus small amount of black, gray, and white

Size H/8 (5 mm) crochet hook

Toilet paper roll

2 yellow animal eyes, 18 mm

Fiberfill stuffing

Disappearing ink marking pen

Pencil

Stitch marker

Yarn needle

BODY

Make Basic Roll Cover (see page 17) using gray yarn for Rnds 1-8 of Top and orange yarn for the remainder.

HOOD

With orange yarn, ch 2.

Row 1: 3 sc in 2nd ch from hook.

Row 2: ch 1, turn, 2 sc in next 3 sts (6 sts).

Row 3: ch 1, turn, *sc in next st, 2 sc in next st* 3 times (9 sts).

Row 4: ch 1, turn, *sc in next 2 sts, 2 sc in next st* 3 times (12 sts).

Row 5: ch 1, turn, *sc in next 3 sts, 2 sc in next st* 3 times (15 sts).

Row 6: ch 1, turn, *sc in next 4 sts, 2 sc in next st* 3 times (18 sts).

Row 7: ch 1, turn, *sc in next 5 sts, 2 sc in next st* 3 times (21 sts).

Row 8: ch 1, turn, *sc in next 6 sts, 2 sc in next st* 3 times (24 sts).

Row 9: ch 1, turn, *sc in next 7 sts, 2 sc in next st* 3 times (27 sts).

Row 10: ch 1, turn, *sc in next 8 sts, 2 sc in next st* 3 times (30 sts).

Note: Change to working in rnds.

Rnds 11-18: sc in each st around. Place marker for beginning of rnd and move marker up as each rnd is completed (50 sts). Fasten off with long tail.

HEADLIGHT (MAKE 2)

With white yarn, make a magic ring, ch 1.

Rnd 1: 6 sc in ring, pull ring almost tight, leaving space to insert post of eye (6 sts).

Rnd 2: 2 sc in each st around (12 sts).

Sl st in next st. Fasten off. Weave in ends.

TIRE (MAKE 4)

Tire is worked in back loops only.

With gray yarn, make a magic ring, ch 1.

Rnd 1: 6 sc in ring, pull ring closed tight (6 sts).

Rnd 2: 2 sc in each st around. Place marker for beginning of rnd and move marker up as each rnd is completed (12 sts).

Rnd 3: *sc in next st, 2 sc in next st* 6 times; change to black yarn in last st (18 sts).

Rnd 4: *sc in next 2 sts, 2 sc in next st* 6 times (24 sts).

Rnd 5: *sc in next 3 sts, 2 sc in next st* 6 times (30 sts).

Rnds 6-7: sc in each st around.

Rnd 8: *sc in next 3 sts, sc2tog* 6 times (24 sts).

Rnd 9: *sc in next 2 sts, sc2tog* 6 times (18 sts).

Rnd 10: *sc in next st, sc2tog* 6 times (12 sts). Stuff piece lightly.

Rnd 11: *sc2tog* 6 times (6 sts).

Fasten off with long tail. Pack more stuffing through opening using eraser end of pencil. Sew hole closed.

GRILLE

With gray yarn, embroider Grille on front of hood, stitching in grooves between rnds. Sew with running stitch, then sew in opposite direction to fill in the spaces, inserting needle through a bit of the stitches on either side to avoid gaps (see template at right).

ASSEMBLY

Insert stem of eyes through center of Headlights, then through front corners of Hood, and attach. To mark placement for top of Hood, put Body on roll of toilet paper and draw a straight line across center front with disappearing ink marking pen. Sew Hood in place, stuffing as you go. Sew Tires in place. Weave in ends. ♦

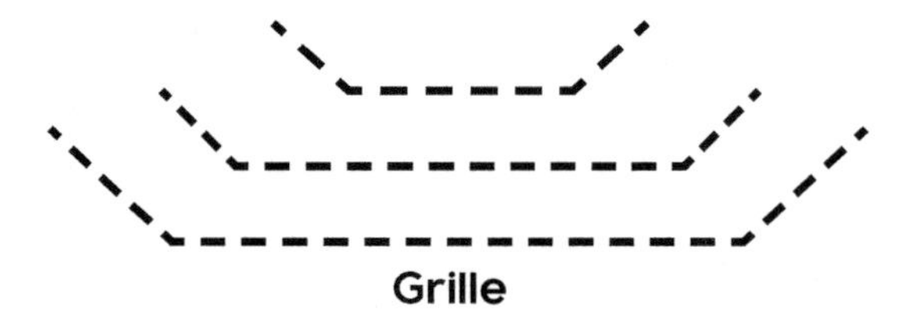
Grille

Stephen Stegosaurus

SUPPLIES

- Worsted weight yarn in blue (approx. 170 yards), gold (approx. 75 yards) and small amount of white and black
- Size H/8 (5 mm) crochet hook
- Toilet paper roll
- 2 yellow animal eyes, 15 mm
- Disappearing ink marking pen
- Fiberfill stuffing
- Stitch marker
- Yarn needle

BODY

Make Basic Roll Cover (see page 17) using blue yarn.

HEAD

With blue yarn, make a magic ring, ch 1.

Rnd 1: 6 sc in ring, pull ring closed tight (6 sts).

Rnd 2: 2 sc in each st around. Place marker for beginning of rnd and move marker up as each rnd is completed (12 sts).

Rnd 3: *sc in next st, 2 sc in next st* 6 times (18 sts).

Rnds 4-5: sc in each st around.

Rnd 6: *sc in next 2 sts, 2 sc in next st* 6 times (24 sts).

Rnds 7-8: sc in each st around.

Rnd 9: *sc in next 3 sts, 2 sc in next st* 6 times (30 sts).

Rnds 10-11: sc in each st around.

Rnd 12: *sc in next 4 sts, 2 sc in next st* 6 times (36 sts).

Rnds 13-14: sc in each st around.

Rnd 15: *sc in next 5 sts, 2 sc in next st* 6 times (42 sts).

Rnds 16-17: sc in each st around.

Fasten off with long tail.

SMALL PLATE (MAKE 2)

With gold yarn, make a magic ring, ch 1.

Rnd 1: 6 sc in ring, pull ring closed tight (6 sts).

Rnd 2: *sc in next 2 sts, 2 sc in next st* 2 times. Place marker for beginning of rnd and move marker up as each rnd is completed (8 sts).

Rnd 3: sc in each st around.

Rnd 4: *sc in next 2 sts, sc2tog* 2 times (6 sts).

Sl st in next st. Fasten off with long tail. Pinch tip into a nice point.

MEDIUM PLATE (MAKE 6)

With gold yarn, make a magic ring, ch 1.

Rnd 1: 6 sc in ring, pull ring closed tight (6 sts).

Rnd 2: *sc in next 2 sts, 2 sc in next st* 2 times. Place marker for beginning of rnd and move marker up as each rnd is completed (8 sts).

Rnd 3: *sc in next 3 sts, 2 sc in next st* 2 times (10 sts).

Rnd 4: *sc in next 4 sts, 2 sc in next st* 2 times (12 sts).

Rnd 5: sc in each st around.

Rnd 6: *sc in next 4 sts, sc2tog* 2 times (10 sts).

Rnd 7: *sc in next 3 sts, sc2tog* 2 times (8 sts).

Sl st in next st. Fasten off with long tail. Pinch tip into a nice point.

LARGE PLATE (MAKE 2)

With gold yarn, make a magic ring, ch 1.

Rnd 1: 6 sc in ring, pull ring closed tight (6 sts).

Rnd 2: *sc in next 2 sts, 2 sc in next st* 2 times. Place marker for beginning of rnd and move marker up as each rnd is completed (8 sts).

Rnd 3: *sc in next 3 sts, 2 sc in next st* 2 times (10 sts).

Rnd 4: *sc in next 4 sts, 2 sc in next st* 2 times (12 sts).

Rnd 5: *sc in next 5 sts, 2 sc in next st* 2 times (14 sts).

Rnd 6: *sc in next 6 sts, 2 sc in next st* 2 times (16 sts).

Rnd 7: *sc in next 7 sts, 2 sc in next st* 2 times (18 sts).

Rnd 8: sc in each st around.

Rnd 9: *sc in next 7 sts, sc2tog* 2 times (16 sts).

Rnd 10: *sc in next 6 sts, sc2tog* 2 times (14 sts).

Rnd 11: *sc in next 5 sts, sc2tog* 2 times (12 sts).

Rnd 12: *sc in next 4 sts, sc2tog* 2 times (10 sts).

Sl st in next st. Fasten off with long tail. Pinch tip into a nice point.

OUTER EYE (MAKE 2)

With white yarn, make a magic ring, ch 1.

Rnd 1: 6 sc in ring, pull ring closed almost tight, leaving room to insert post of eye (6 sts).

Rnd 2: 2 sc in each st around. Place marker for beginning of rnd and move marker up as each rnd is completed (12 sts).

Rnds 3-4: sc in each st around.

Fasten off with long tail.

EYELID (MAKE 2)

With blue yarn, ch 2.

Row 1: 3 sc in 2nd ch from hook.

Row 2: ch 1, turn, 2 sc in next 3 sts (6 sts).

Row 3: ch 1, turn, *sc in next st, 2 sc in next st* 3 times (9 sts).

Row 4: ch 1, turn, *sc in next 2 sts, 2 sc in next st* 3 times (12 sts).

Fasten off with long tail. Weave in short tail from starting point.

LEG (MAKE 4)

With blue yarn, make a magic ring, ch 1.

Rnd 1: 6 sc in ring, pull ring closed tight (6 sts).

Rnd 2: 2 sc in each st around. Place marker for beginning of rnd and move marker up as each rnd is completed (12 sts).

Rnd 3: *sc in next st, 2 sc in next st* 6 times (18 sts).

Rnds 4-8: sc in each st around.

Sl st in next st. Fasten off with long tail. With a double strand of gold yarn, embroider toenails by making 5 French knots in front Legs and 3 French knots in back Legs, stitching in the gutter between Rnds 3 and 4.

ASSEMBLY

Lay Body down flat and draw a line with disappearing ink marking pen from center back to center front (see Figure A). Starting at back of Body, sew Plates in 2 rows on each side of line in this order: 1 Medium Plate, 1 Large Plate, 2 Medium Plates and 1 Small Plate. Attach animal eyes to center of Outer Eyes. Stuff Eyes and sew to Head. Place Eyelids so that straight side angles across Eyes and sew in position. With a double strand of black yarn, embroider 2 French knots for Nostrils. Stuff Head lightly, flatten, and sew the open end closed. Sew Head to Body. Mark position of Legs with Leg Templates (see page 90). Stuff Legs and sew to Body. Weave in ends. ♦

FIGURE A

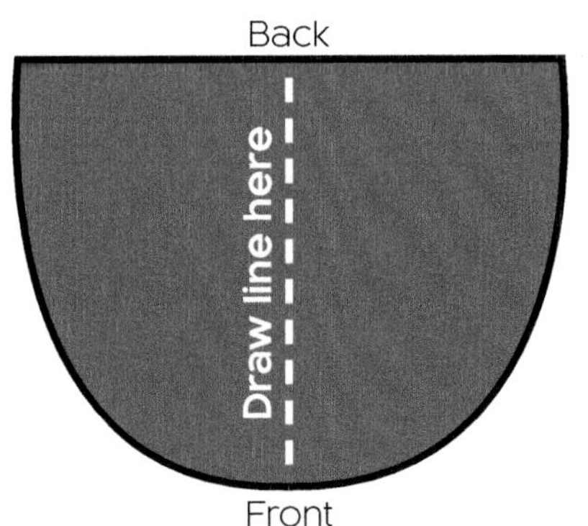

Sheldon Sheep

SUPPLIES

Worsted weight yarn in off-white (approx. 200 yards) and small amount of black

Size H/8 (5 mm) crochet hook

Toilet paper roll

2 black buttons, 1/2" diameter

Fiberfill stuffing

Disappearing ink marking pen

Stitch marker

Yarn needle

HEAD AND BODY

The Sides are crocheted with Loop Stitch (lp st). Note: The loops will form on the underside of your work.

With off-white yarn, sc Top of Basic Roll Cover (see page 17). For Sides, ch 1, flip Top to the wrong side and crochet with lp st. Turn work when done so that right side of face and loops are on the outside.

EAR (MAKE 2)

With off-white yarn, make a magic ring, ch 1.

Rnd 1: 6 sc in ring, pull ring closed tight (6 sts).

Rnd 2: *sc in next 2 sts, 2 sc in next st* 2 times. Place marker for beginning of rnd and move marker up as each rnd is completed (8 sts).

Rnd 3: *sc in next 3 sts, 2 sc in next st" 2 times (10 sts).

Rnd 4: *sc in next 4 sts, 2 sc in next st" 2 times (12 sts).

Rnd 5: *sc in next 5 sts, 2 sc in next st" 2 times (14 sts).

Rnd 6: *sc in next 6 sts, 2 sc in next st" 2 times (16 sts).

Rnd 7: sc in each st around.

Rnd 8: *sc in next 6 sts, sc2tog* 2 times (14 sts).

Rnd 9: *sc in next 5 sts, sc2tog* 2 times (12 sts).

Rnd 10: *sc in next 4 sts, sc2tog* 2 times (10 sts).

Rnd 11: *sc in next 3 sts, sc2tog* 2 times (8 sts).

Sl st in next st. Fasten off with long tail.

LEG (MAKE 4)

With off-white yarn, make a magic ring, ch 1.

Rnd 1: 6 sc in ring, pull ring closed tight (6 sts).

Rnd 2: 2 sc in each st around. Place marker for beginning of rnd and move marker up as each rnd is completed (12 sts).

Rnd 3: *sc in next st, 2 sc in next st* 6 times (18 sts).

Rnds 4-8: sc in each st around.

Sl st in next st. Fasten off with long tail.

SNOUT

With off-white yarn, make a magic ring, ch 1.

Rnd 1: 6 sc in ring, pull ring closed tight (6 sts).

Rnd 2: 2 sc in each st around. Place marker for beginning of rnd and move marker up as each rnd is completed (12 sts).

Rnd 3: *sc in next st, 2 sc in next st* 6 times (18 sts).

Rnd 4: *sc in next 2 sts, 2 sc in next st* 6 times (24 sts).

Rnds 5-6: sc in each st around.

Sl st in next st. Fasten off with long tail.

ASSEMBLY

With black yarn, embroider nose and mouth on Snout. Stuff Snout. Sew Snout and button eyes to face. Sew Ears to Body. Mark position of Legs with Leg Templates (see page 90). Stuff Legs and sew to Body. Weave in ends. ♦

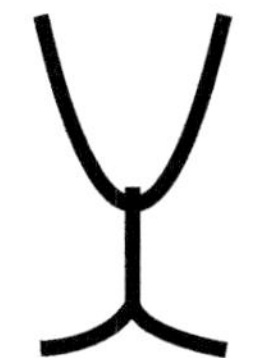

Nose & Mouth

Santa Hat

SUPPLIES

Worsted weight yarn in red (approx. 100 yards) and white (approx. 50 yards). A fuzzy white yarn is best.

Size H/8 (5 mm) crochet hook

Toilet paper roll

Small piece of cardboard

Stitch marker

Yarn needle

Stiff hair brush (optional)

HAT

With red yarn, make a magic ring, ch 1.

Rnd 1: 6 sc in ring, pull ring closed tight (6 sts).

Rnd 2: 2 sc in each st around. Place marker for beginning of rnd and move marker up as each rnd is completed (12 sts).

Rnds 3-4: sc in each st around.

Rnd 5: *sc in next st, 2 sc in next st* 6 times (18 sts).

Rnds 6-7: sc in each st around.

Rnd 8: *sc in next 2 sts, 2 sc in next st* 6 times (24 sts).

Rnds 9-11: sc in each st around.

Rnd 12: *sc in next 3 sts, 2 sc in next st* 6 times (30 sts).

Rnds 13-15: sc in each st around.

Rnd 16: *sc in next 4 sts, 2 sc in next st* 6 times (36 sts).

Rnds 17-19: sc in each st around.

Rnd 20: *sc in next 5 sts, 2 sc in next st* 6 times (42 sts).

Rnds 21-24: sc in each st around.

Rnd 25: *sc in next 6 sts, 2 sc in next st* 6 times (48 sts).

Rnds 26-29: sc in each st around.

Rnd 30: *sc in next 7 sts, 2 sc in next st* 6 times (54 sts).

Rnds 31-34: sc in each st around.

Rnd 35: *sc in next 8 sts, 2 sc in next st* 6 times (60 sts).

Fitting your Hat: At this point, the diameter of the open end should be similar to the diameter of your TP roll. The match doesn't need to be exact. If your opening is way too large, rip your stitches back to a good fit and continue at Rnd 36. If your opening is way too small, repeat Rnd 35, increasing the number of plain sc ("sc in next ___ sts") by 1 st for each rnd until proper diameter is reached and continue at Rnd 36.

Rnds 36-50: sc in each st around; change to white yarn in last st.

Rnds 51-?: sc in each st around until white measures 3" from red section. Sl st in next st. Fasten off.

POM POM

Cut a rectangle of cardboard measuring 2" x 6". Wrap white yarn widthwise around the cardboard 75 times. Carefully slide yarn off cardboard. Using a scrap of yarn, tie bundle together tightly around the middle. Cut loops open. Fluff Pom Pom and trim ends into a nice round shape.

ASSEMBLY

Tie Pom Pom to end of Hat. Roll up brim 1½ inches. Weave in ends. Brush white brim & Pom Pom with stiff hair brush to create a fuzzier appearance, if desired. ♦

Trina Triceratops

SUPPLIES

Worsted weight yarn in green (approx. 170 yards) and small amount of tan

Size H/8 (5 mm) crochet hook

Toilet paper roll

2 yellow animal eyes, 15 mm

Disappearing ink marking pen

Fiberfill stuffing

Stitch marker

Yarn needle

HEAD AND BODY

Make Basic Roll Cover (see page 17) using green yarn and working Rnd 3 of Sides in back loops only. Resume working in both loops for Rnds 4 and beyond.

FRILL

The top of the Basic Roll Cover forms a hexagon. On the rnd of unworked front loops (Rnd 3 of Basic Roll Cover Sides), place a stitch marker at one of the hexagon's points (see red dot on diagram). Count 20 stitches to the right of stitch marker. This is where you will begin stitching the Frill.

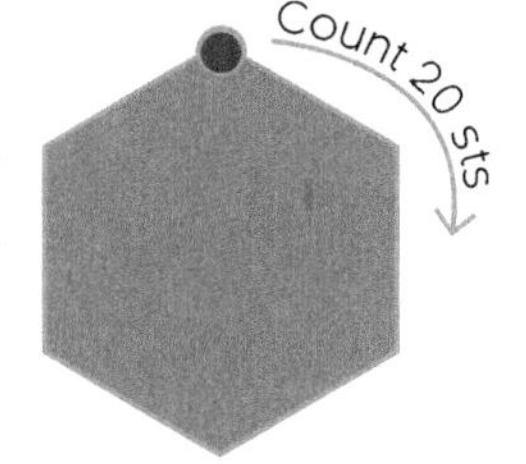

With green yarn, fasten on.

Row 1: *sc in next 9 sts, 2 sc in next st* 4 times (44 sts).

Row 2: ch 1, turn, *sc in next 10 sts, 2 sc in next st* 4 times (48 sts).

Row 3: ch 1, turn, *sc in next 11 sts, 2 sc in next st* 4 times (52 sts).

Row 4: ch 1, turn, *sc in next 12 sts, 2 sc in next st* 4 times (56 sts).

Row 5: ch 1, turn, *sc in next 13 sts, 2 sc in next st* 4 times (60 sts).

Row 6: ch 1, turn, *sc in next 14 sts, 2 sc in next st* 4 times; change to tan yarn in last st (64 sts).

Row 7: ch 1, turn, *3 sc in 1st st, ch 2, sc in 2nd ch from hook, 2 more sc in 1st st, skip next st, sl st in next st* across. Fasten off.

LEG (MAKE 4)

With green, make magic ring, ch 1.

Rnd 1: 6 sc in ring, pull ring closed tight (6 sts).

Rnd 2: 2 sc in each st around. Place marker for beginning of rnd and move marker up as each rnd is completed (12 sts).

Rnd 3: *sc in next st, 2 sc in next st* 6 times (18 sts).

Rnds 4-8: sc in each st around.

Sl st in next st. Fasten off with long tail. With a double strand of tan yarn, embroider toenails by making 5 French knots in front Legs and 4 French knots in back Legs, stitching in the gutter between Rnds 3 and 4.

HORN (MAKE 3)

With tan yarn, make magic ring, ch 1.

Rnd 1: 4 sc in ring, pull ring closed tight (4 sts).

Rnd 2: *sc in next st, 2 sc in next st* 2 times. Place marker for beginning of rnd and move marker up as each rnd is completed (6 sts).

Rnd 3: sc in each st around.

Rnd 4: *sc in next 2 sts, 2 sc in next st* 2 times (8 sts).

Rnd 5: sc in each st around.

Rnd 6: *sc in next 3 sts, 2 sc in next st* 2 times (10 sts).

Rnd 7: sc in each st around.

Rnd 8: *sc in next 4 sts, 2 sc in next st* 2 times (12 sts).

Rnds 9-11: sc in each st around.

Sl st in next st. Fasten off with long tail.

ASSEMBLY

Attach eyes, clipping off excess stem with wire cutters. Stuff Horns and sew to face. Mark position of Legs with Leg Templates (see page 90). Stuff Legs and sew to Body. Weave in ends. ♦

Sunflower

SUPPLIES

Worsted weight yarn in green (approx. 75 yards), brown (approx. 25 yards) and yellow (approx. 135 yards).

Size H/8 (5 mm) crochet hook

Toilet paper roll

Stitch marker

Yarn needle

CENTER AND STEM

Make Basic Roll Cover (see page 17) using brown yarn for Top and Rnds 1-2 of Sides. Finish Sides with green yarn.

PETAL (MAKE 18)

With yellow yarn, make a magic ring, ch 1.

Rnd 1: 6 sc in ring, pull ring closed tight (6 sts).

Rnd 2: *sc in next 2 sts, 2 sc in next st* 2 times. Place marker for beginning of rnd and move marker up as each rnd is completed (8 sts).

Rnd 3: *sc in next 3 sts, 2 sc in next st* 2 times (10 sts).

Rnd 4: *sc in next 4 sts, 2 sc in next st* 2 times (12 sts).

Rnds 5-10: sc in each st around.

Sl st in next st. Fasten off with long tail. Fold lower end of petal in half so that corners meet and stitch to secure.

ASSEMBLY

Sew Petals in place around rim of brown circle. Weave in ends. ♦

Maggie Dog

SUPPLIES

- Worsted weight yarn in tan fleck (approx. 175 yards) and small amount of brown fleck
- Size H/8 (5 mm) crochet hook
- Toilet paper roll
- 2 black animal eyes, 15 mm
- 1 triangle animal nose, 21 mm
- Disappearing ink marking pen
- Small piece of cardboard
- Fiberfill stuffing
- Stitch marker
- Yarn needle
- Socket wrench (optional)

HEAD AND BODY

Make Basic Roll Cover (see page 17) using tan fleck yarn.

SNOUT

Cut a square of cardboard measuring 4" x 4". Wrap tan fleck yarn around cardboard 50 times. Carefully slide yarn off cardboard. Using a scrap of matching yarn, tie bundle together tightly around the middle. Cut loops open. Flatten pom pom so that all strands radiate from the center (See Figure A) and set aside.

EAR (MAKE 2)

Cut a rectangle of cardboard measuring 3" x 9". Wrap brown fleck yarn lengthwise around cardboard 12 times. Carefully slide yarn off cardboard. Using a scrap of matching yarn, tie bundle together tightly around the middle. Cut loops open.

LEG (MAKE 4)

With tan fleck yarn, make a magic ring, ch 1.

Rnd 1: 6 sc in ring, pull ring closed tight (6 sts).

Rnd 2: 2 sc in each st around. Place marker for beginning of rnd and move marker up as each rnd is completed (12 sts).

Rnd 3: *sc in next st, 2 sc in next st* 6 times (18 sts).

Rnds 4-8: sc in each st around.

Sl st in next st. Fasten off with long tail.

Insert nose here

FIGURE A

TAIL

With tan fleck yarn, make a magic ring, ch 1.

Rnd 1: 4 sc in ring, pull ring closed tight (4 sts).

Rnd 2: *sc in next st, 2 sc in next st* 2 times. Place marker for beginning of rnd and move marker up as each rnd is completed (6 sts).

Rnd 3: sc in each st around.

Rnd 4: *sc in next 2 sts, 2 sc in next st* 2 times (8 sts).

Rnds 5-9: sc in each st around.

Sl st in next st. Fasten off with long tail.

ASSEMBLY

To attach Snout, insert post of nose through center of pom pom (See Figure A) and then through center of face. Check front of face to be sure nose is positioned properly. Place washer on post and press to attach. Note: Use a socket wrench for assistance (see page 9). Attach eyes, clipping off excess stem with wire cutters. For eyebrows, embroider 5 straight stitches with tan fleck yarn over each eye (see Eyebrow Guide). Tie Ears to top of Head. Mark position of Legs with Leg Templates (see page 90). Stuff Legs and sew to Body. Stuff Tail and sew to Body. Trim stray strands on Snout and Ears. Weave in ends. ♦

Choo Choo Train

SUPPLIES

Worsted weight yarn in gray (approx. 70 yards), raspberry (approx. 45 yards), black (approx. 25 yards) and small amount of white

Size H/8 (5 mm) crochet hook

Toilet paper roll

Fiberfill stuffing

2 black buttons, 1/2" diameter (optional)

Stitch marker

Yarn needle

ENGINE

Make Basic Roll Cover (see page 17) with gray yarn for Top and Rnds 1-4 of Sides, black yarn for Rnds 5-10 of Sides, and raspberry yarn to the end.

SMOKE STACK

With gray yarn, make a magic ring, ch 1.

Rnd 1: 5 sc in ring, pull ring closed tight (5 sts).

Rnd 2: 2 sc in each st around; change to black yarn in last st (10 sts).

Rnds 3-?: sc in each st around until piece is 2" long.

Sl st in next st. Fasten off with long tail.

OUTER EYE (MAKE 2)

With white yarn, make a magic ring, ch 1.

Rnd 1: 6 sc in ring, pull ring closed tight (6 sts).

Rnd 2: 2 sc in each st around. Place marker for beginning of rnd and move marker up as each rnd is completed (12 sts).

Rnd 3: *sc in next st, 2 sc in next st* 6 times (18 sts).

Sl st in next st. Fasten off with long tail.

INNER EYE (MAKE 2)

Use buttons or crochet as follows.

With black yarn, make a magic ring, ch 1.

Rnd 1: 5 sc in ring, pull ring closed tight (5 sts).

Sl st in next st. Fasten off with long tail.

NOSE

With gray yarn, make a magic ring, ch 1.

Rnd 1: 4 sc in ring, pull ring closed tight (4 sts).

Rnd 2: sc in next 3 sts, 2 sc in next st. Place marker for beginning of rnd and move marker up as each rnd is completed (5 sts).

Rnd 3: sc in next 4 sts, 2 sc in next st (6 sts).

Rnd 4: sc in next 5 sts, 2 sc in next st (7 sts).

Fasten off with long tail.

WHEEL (MAKE 6)

Wheel is worked in back loops only.

With gray yarn, make a magic ring, ch 1.

Rnd 1: 6 sc in ring, pull ring closed tight (6 sts).

Rnd 2: 2 sc in each st around. Place marker for beginning of rnd and move marker up as each rnd is completed (12 sts).

Rnd 3: *sc in next st, 2 sc in next st* 6 times (18 sts).

Rnd 4: sc in each st around.

Rnd 5: *sc in next st, sc2tog in next st* 6 times (12 sts).

Rnd 6: sc2tog 6 times (6 sts).

Fasten off with long tail. Flatten piece and sew opening closed tight. Weave in end.

MOUTH

With raspberry yarn, ch 9.

Row 1: starting in 2nd ch from hook sc2tog, sc in next 4 sts, sc2tog (6 sts).

Row 2: ch 1, turn, sc2tog, sc in next 2 sts, sc2tog (4 sts).

Row 3: ch 1, turn, sc2tog, sc2tog (2 sts).

Row 4: ch 1, turn, sc2tog (1 st).

Fasten off with long tail. Pinch and pull corners to shape piece into a nice triangle. Weave loose end through wrong side of work to fill in any gaps.

SIDE ROD (MAKE 2)

With black yarn, ch st until chain measures 3 1/2" long. Fasten off with long tail.

ASSEMBLY

Place 3 Wheels side-by-side. Lay Side Rod on top of wheels, just above center. Sew Side Rod in place. Repeat with remaining 3 Wheels. Put Engine on roll of toilet paper and pin Wheel assemblies in place. Sew top third of Wheels to Engine so that bottom of each Wheel hangs free. Stuff Nose and sew to center of face. Stuff Smoke Stack and sew to Engine. Sew Inner Eyes to Outer Eyes, off center, then sew Eyes to face. Sew Mouth in place. With black yarn, embroider straight stitch eyebrows. Weave in ends. ♦

Choo! Choo!

Copy the templates at 100 percent.

Busy Bee

mouth, page 23

Francesca & Frankie Frog

mouth, page 27

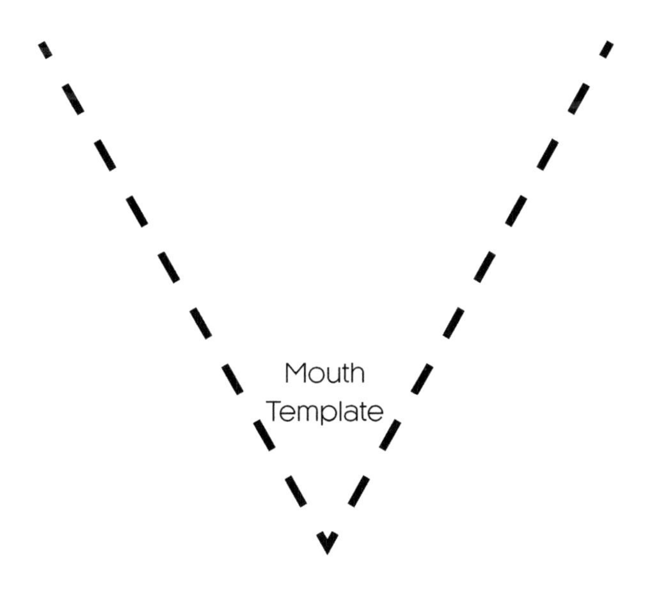

Leg Templates

Leo Lion, page 29; Kitty Cat, page 51; Peggy Pig, page 57; Simon Cow, page 60; Stephen Stegosaurus, page 75; Sheldon Sheep, page 77; Trina Triceratops, page 81 and Maggie Dog, page 85.

Leg Template

To mark Leg placement, copy and cut out 4 Leg Templates.
Pin in position to Body.
Trace with Disappearing Ink Marking Pen.

Leg Template

To mark Leg placement, copy and cut out 4 Leg Templates.
Pin in position to Body.
Trace with Disappearing Ink Marking Pen.

Leg Template

To mark Leg placement, copy and cut out 4 Leg Templates.
Pin in position to Body.
Trace with Disappearing Ink Marking Pen.

Leg Template

To mark Leg placement, copy and cut out 4 Leg Templates.
Pin in position to Body.
Trace with Disappearing Ink Marking Pen.

Party Cake

scallops, page 35

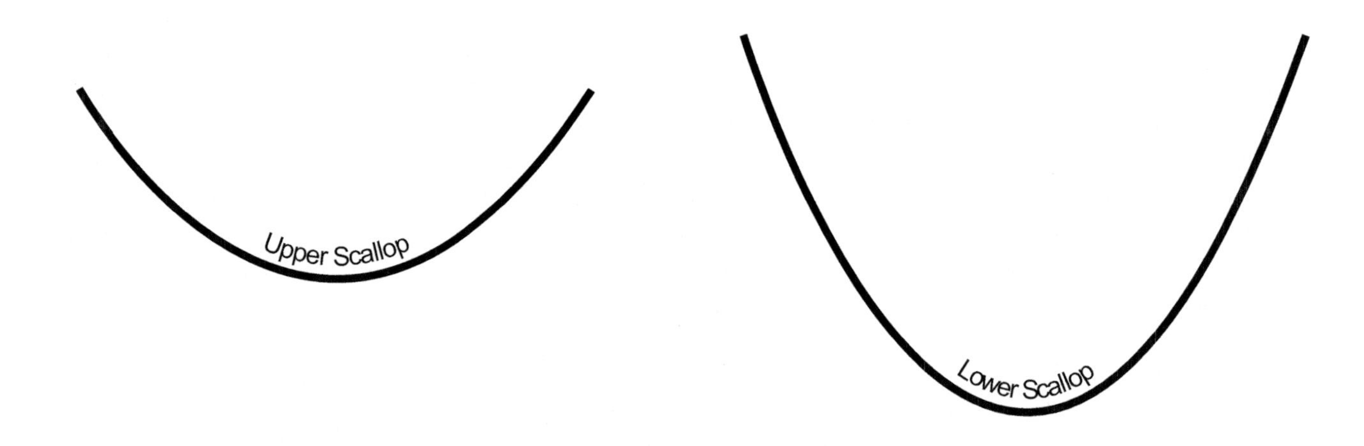

Alan the Alien

mouth, page 39

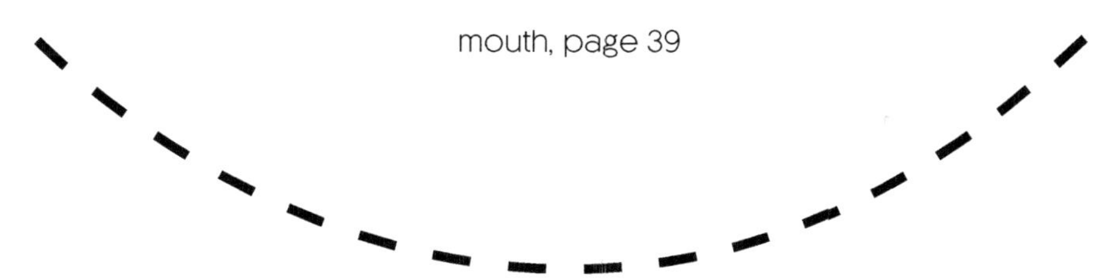

Jack O'Lantern

mouth, page 41

Snowman Sam

arms, page 47

Teddy Bear

arm and leg templates, page 63

Arm Template
To mark Arm placement, copy and cut out 2 Arm Templates. Pin in position to Body. Trace with Disappearing Ink Marking Pen.

Arm Template
To mark Arm placement, copy and cut out 2 Arm Templates. Pin in position to Body. Trace with Disappearing Ink Marking Pen.

Leg Template
To mark Leg placement, copy and cut out 2 Leg Templates. Pin in position to Body. Trace with Disappearing Ink Marking Pen.

Leg Template
To mark Leg placement, copy and cut out 2 Leg Templates. Pin in position to Body. Trace with Disappearing Ink Marking Pen.

Bunny Rabbit

mouth, page 67

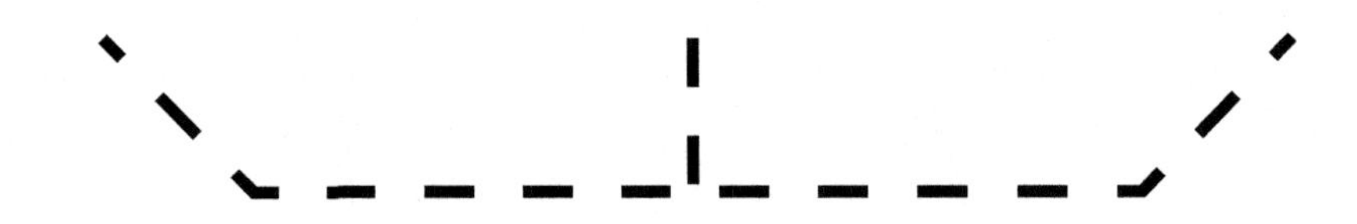

ReSources

YARN

Caron Yarn
caron.com
Simply Soft

Lion Brand
lionbrand.com
Vanna's Choice
Cotton Ease

Red Heart
redheart.com
Soft Yarn

Hobby Lobby
shop.hobbylobby.com
I Love This Yarn

Michaels
michaels.com
Loops & Threads *Impeccable*
Loops & Threads *Soft & Shiny*

Joann Fabric and Craft Stores
joann.com
Caron *Simply Soft*
Caron *Natura*
Lion Brand *Vanna's Choice*
Lion Brand *Cotton Ease*
Red Heart *Soft Yarn*

SAFETY EYES & NOSES

Amazon
amazon.com

CR's Crafts
crscrafts.com

Etsy Shop 6060
etsy.com/shop/6060

Glass Eyes Online
glasseyesonline.com

NOTIONS

Joann Fabric and Craft Stores
joann.com
Clover *Soft Touch Crochet Hook*
Jumbo tapestry needles
Locking stitch markers
Fiberfill stuffing
Knitting counter

STITCH TUTORIALS

YouTube!
youtube.com
Search on the name of the stitch or technique you want to learn.

Pinterest
pinterest.com/LindalooEnt/
Visit my Pinterest page to view video tutorials for the stitches and techniques used in this book. Look for the boards named "Amigurumi Tutorials" and "Embroidery Tutorials".

May your life be long and useful . . .
like a roll of toilet paper.

Other books by LINDA WRIGHT

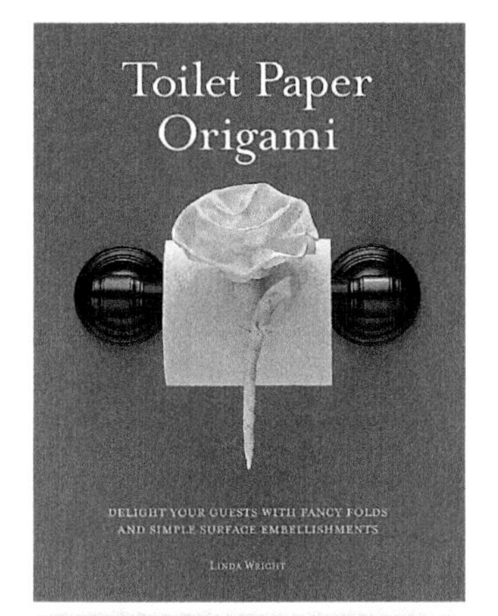

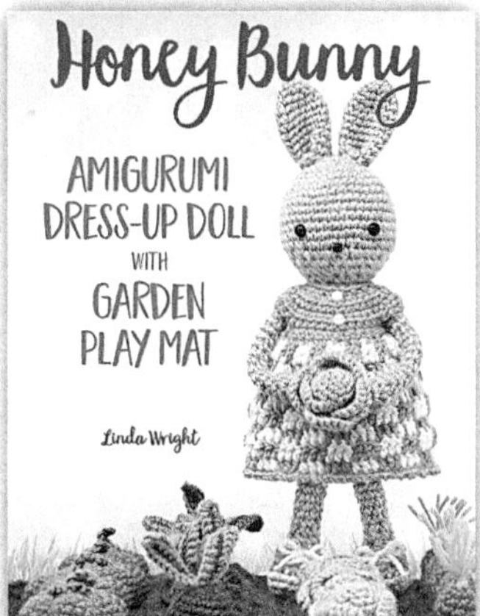

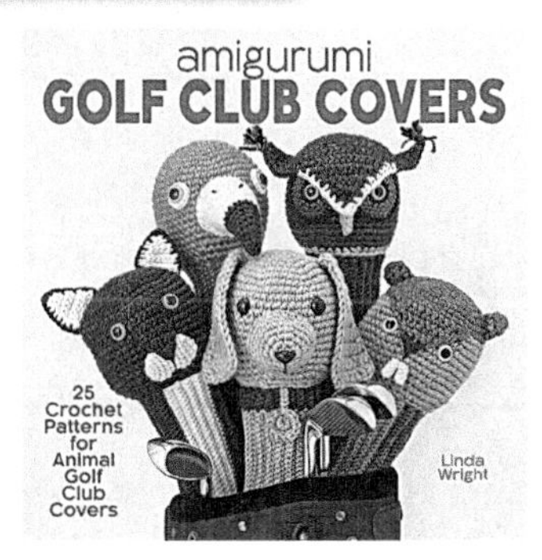

LINDA WRIGHT studied textiles and clothing design at the Pennsylvania State University. She is the author of various handicraft books including the groundbreaking *Toilet Paper Origami*, its companion book, *Toilet Paper Origami On a Roll* and numerous works of amigurumi-style crochet. To learn more about these fun-filled books, visit:

amazon.com/author/lindawright **instagram.com/tporigami** **pinterest.com/LindalooEnt**

Printed in Great Britain
by Amazon